A FOUNDING FATHERS' VOTING GUIDE

- A DAILY READER -

COMPILED AND PARAPHRASED BY

DAVID A. HEBERT

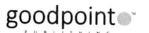

goodpoint™
PUBLISHING

365: A Founding Fathers' Voting Guide [A Daily Reader]

© 2014 GoodPoint Publishing

Published by GoodPoint Publishing
A Division of GoodPoint Elite Communication
Plover (Stevens Point), WI 54467

Printed by DigiCOPY, Stevens Point, WI

Cover design: Dave Hebert
Cover image: licensed (morguefile.com/creative/wintersixfour)
Interior design and typeset: GoodPoint Publishing

Resources: Please view the list of resources at our web site: www.365founders.us.

Library of Congress Cataloging-in-Publication-Data
PCN Number: 2014913599
Hebert, David A.
365: A Founding Fathers' Voting Guide / David A. Hebert.
   Pages cm.
Includes bibliographical references
ISBN-13:978-0-9906344-0-9

Title.

WITH GRATITUDE:

No project of this magnitude can be completed without the help, inspiration and advice of others. To those who assisted in this effort, I offer my heartfelt thanks.

My appreciation is due the many teachers, authors, speakers and producers of history-genre documentaries and films that have stirred and focused my interest in these topics and given me a lasting admiration for our founding fathers and their timeless wisdom.

I extend my thanks, also, to my precious sister, Marilyn Santiago, for her encouraging words and insightful comments throughout this process. And to Rick Santiago, I can't say enough how I enjoy and gain from our times bouncing ideas off of one another. John Jordens, Frank Szalai, Ken Knapp, Michael Aavang, Betty Barnes, Kevin and Jamison Briscoe, Camille Solberg and others have supplied personal support and encouragement, keeping me on track.

Professor Wade Mahon contributed immensely by providing his considerable expertise with the language and rhetorical patterns of the subject era as well as his perceptive suggestions and sharp eye. Monica Anderson also lent a keen eye to bring many errors to my reluctant attention. Craig Shuler generously gave of his professional expertise, as did Shelly Martin, Nicky Brillowski and Jenny Larsen.

A very special "thank you" is owed to my former neighbor, longtime friend and, now, governor Scott Walker, for making time in the midst of a daunting schedule to review the book and add his gracious foreword. Senator Ron Johnson (R-WI) has also kindly offered his encouragement and endorsement.

My eternal and loving gratitude goes to my wife, Barbara, and my children Danni and Matt, for allowing me time away from them, fastened to my Macintosh and web browser, to pursue this dream.

Finally, I would have neither the tenacity nor patience to complete a project like this without my Source of light and freedom, Jesus Christ, and the scriptures that instruct and inspire me daily.

My heartfelt thanks to you all.

DAVE

TO THE READER:

As with many books in the historical genre, some practices in word choice have been adopted which may differ from preferred contemporary styles. This brief summary addresses some of those choices as well as other content in this book.

Paraphrasing

Personal pronouns are paraphrased in the masculine voice, except where the original quotation may have implied the feminine. This was the typical manner used in the culture of the times described.

Whenever the exact words and source of the original quote were available, I sought to replicate the author's intended meaning; when differences in the precise quotation occur among various sources, the more contemporary phrasing was used.

No one, certainly not this editor, can match the elegance, passion or wisdom of the original authors. This edition dares to offer the reader a paraphrased version of most quotations included (except when the meaning of the original is clear to modern ears) only as a convenience in better understanding and applying these 18th- and 19th-century statements to our times and vocabulary. Nothing more.

Paraphrasing was not intended merely to substitute words from their time with ours. Meanings, of course, are of prime importance (as best they could be determined from the best research available to this editor). Some words, phrases and terms were chosen simply to provide a different or broader perspective on the original, others to include a wider, though potentially unfamiliar, audience. Some readers may reasonably disagree with the choices made. Nevertheless, I trust you will find the paraphrased versions enlightening and thought-provoking.

Note: All authors quoted in this work are described in summary in Appendix A. Where applicable, proper titles of authors listed in the paraphrased text are based on the best current understanding of their position at the time of the quoted writing or speech.

(Note: The idioms, spelling, punctuation and style of the founders may look to us as typos. In this book, however, that is not the case.)

Selecting Content

In selecting the content you're about to read, I attempted to find a variety of authors to quote. What I found is that many lesser-known founding fathers were far less quotable—or at least less memorable—than many of the men we are most familiar with. As a result, fewer of their words were collected and preserved for the benefit of future audiences.

Because of the fame and stature of those who had led the efforts at resistance to British rule in the colonies—and the resulting revolution and writing of the Constitution—their writings, speeches and political records are more readily available than those of their contemporaries, which explains a somewhat limited, though illustrious, roster of authors.

Some readers may also notice that certain founder's words may appear to be clustered close together in the daily entries. Since the readings are categorized by topic, such proximity may indicate areas of interest or urgency. Note, also, that many quotes would fit well into more than one category. In any case, their literary legacies greatly enrich us, their readers.

The authenticity of a few quotes is challenged regarding authorship, date, source, etc. While these may not be as certain as you or I would prefer, those that are considered particularly dubious have been left out of this book.

Freedom of Thought

Of course, one of the greatest freedoms sought and secured by these men was the freedom to disagree. Some of the patriots quoted here were political rivals, even foes. Their words often clashed forcefully and, occasionally, with irreconcilable results. While a few may have vehemently opposed one another, they resolutely stood shoulder-to-shoulder against their common enemies of ignorance, arrogance, tyranny and complacency.

Similarly, because these founders valued freedom to think and to reason without prejudice, they assumed the right to change one's mind. It follows, then, that some of the opinions included here may have evolved from previous views, were overturned in debate by others or were modified or even refuted later in life. Don't let that deter you; all were regarded, at some level, by their contemporaries and generally considered by most as contributing to the relevant debate. We are wise to do the same.

Further Study

It is apparent in our day that not all Americans are ardent readers or students of history. Whether it's a question of time, opportunity or inclination, many today have little informed knowledge of the people, the seasons, the events and the tensions that produced the quotations referenced in this book. That is understood and welcomed. It's my goal to stir within each of us that hidden historian and to pique his/her curiosity with the profound and enticing words of some of America's most able thinkers to such a degree that it will prompt some to study further the founders and their times.

To that end, a list of resources is offered at our web site (365founders.us). Selected general works that can supply background information, dramatic portrayals and/or biographical data is also offered to guide the study of this most significant era in our American experience. These sources were instrumental in helping me to create this work and I highly recommend them to each of you.

Why "A Voting Guide"?

The Merriam-Webster Dictionary defines a *guide* as "someone or something that provides a person with basic guiding information." It can be argued that anything a recognized expert states regarding a subject within his/her scope of expertise is assumed to be a *guiding* maxim—that is, a lesson to be heard, considered and adopted as true or rejected as either untenable or impractical.

In that sense, this book—like other books that accurately reflect the words of the founders regarding the culture and government they collectively built is truly a guide for its readers. They are, after all, the ultimate experts in such areas.

It can further be argued that all American citizens have—by birth or by vow—an inherent obligation to champion the cause of America by actively and knowledgeably participating in the governing of America. For the average American who is neither a politician nor an attorney nor an academic, the premiere exercise of that obligation is the vote. Since the guidance left to us by the founders was entirely for the purpose of creating, building and keeping a strong and free republic, it is presumed that that guidance had as its aim their listeners' wise, informed, intelligent and reasoned votes.

It is in that sense, only, that this book claims to be a "Voting Guide."

In Conclusion

This book is the first in the *Dejavu Series* of daily readers. The series is so named because the content of each title will remind modern readers that history repeats itself, thus giving each generation the opportunity to profit from history's optimism as well as its warnings.

While this work is labeled, "A *Daily* Reader," if you're like me you won't be able to put it down that easily. If you only have time to read and reflect upon one entry each day, this book is for you. But if you prefer to read through at your leisure or to jump around, feel free to do that—it will prove beneficial and satisfying either way.

I freely acknowledge that I am neither a credentialed historian nor a scholar. Like many of you, I am merely a man who enjoys great wisdom and well-crafted words and who wishes to share what he has discovered. That said, any and all errors or misinterpretations in these page are my responsibility. Comments and corrections are always welcome via our website.

Finally, there is no doubt that in these pages many of you will come to know better and more intimately the hopes, anxieties, values and timeless insights of many of the men and women to whom we are all so deeply indebted. I trust you will come away revived, renewed and reinvigorated to preserve our unique, even revolutionary, inheritance.

Enjoy.

DAVID A HEBERT
July 4, 2014

THE TABLE OF CONTENTS

PART II – THE PURSUIT

An American Dignity

(DAYS 76 - 89)

An American Patriotism

(DAYS 90 - 97)

A Moral People

(DAYS 98 - 107)

A Welcome Piety

(DAYS 108 - 132)

PART III – THE GENIUS

On Property and Prosperity

(DAYS 133 - 149)

A Robust Economy

(DAYS 150 - 164)

A Global Trust

(DAYS 165 - 171)

An American Exceptionalism

(DAYS 172 - 184)

On God and Governing

(DAYS 185 - 204)

APPENDIX A: THE AUTHORS

APPENDIX B: THE INDEX

THE FORWARD

365: A Founding Fathers' Voting Guide is a wonderful collection of thoughts from some of the great minds that created this wonderful country we call America. Dave Hebert does an amazing job of collecting these important quotes and translating them into modern conversation without altering the original intent.

One of my favorite sections is Ben Franklin's comment regarding poverty on DAY 133. For years, I've said that true freedom and prosperity does not come from the mighty hand of the government. It comes from empowering people to control their own lives and their own destinies through the dignity of work. Franklin's comments and Dave's modern day translation echo those beliefs. Bravo.

365: A Founding Fathers' Voting Guide is a great read for anyone who values the freedoms we hold dear. It provides a daily reminder to not let those freedoms slip away.

Governor Scott Walker
Wisconsin

THE PREAMBLE

"By learning and understanding history, voters will be better able to expect the future. They will benefit from the experience of people in different periods and countries. They'll become skilled at judging both the actions and intentions of others and prepared to recognize blind ambition, no matter what disguise it wears and, seeing it, to expose it for what it is." *(Thomas Jefferson, Notes on the State of Virginia, Query 14, 1781, paraphrased)*

"You get what you pay for."

An ancient and universal maxim says that value has an associated cost; the greater the value of anything, whether material or spiritual, the higher, and more daunting, the cost. That principle also applies to governments and societies.

America's founders, who conceived and formed the American Ideal, understood that principle, perhaps more than all but a few of their contemporaries and predecessors. And the price they paid to live out their convictions is the stuff of legend.

All nations are guided and governed by leaders administering a system of government of their own choosing. Whether monarchs or proxies, tyrants or saints, free or oppressed, all leaders follow the customs, rules and principles they think best—sometimes for their constituents, too often for themselves and/or their patrons.

The United States of America is so unique and innovative—and, yes, revolutionary—because it is governed solely by principles embodied in the U.S. Constitution, principles that were painstakingly chosen by highly motivated men with keen minds, intense personalities, a sense of divinely favored destiny and the inspiration and insights of dedicated women. These men were flawed but astonishing in their unique ability and determination to create the most liberated, the most independent and the most prosperous society ever established by men. They investigated, studied, analyzed, catalogued, agonized over and debated those characteristics that had historically formed the most efficient, lasting, benevolent and prosperous governments—as well as the most treacherous and most inept.

What was missing from all available models was individual and regional autonomy based on reason, mutual regard and divine (or, natural) rights.

They then tested their findings among families and peers, in neighborhoods and churches, within industry and militias and conventions, by letter and essay and speech and debate. And world history has proven that their eventual solution is, simply, the most secure, humane, productive and free system ever devised by men.

Over the intervening decades between their generation and ours, the incredible wisdom of these founding fathers has earned our utmost respect and devotion. Through dreadful, exuberant and occasionally indifferent times, entire continents have applauded and attempted to mimic their intellectual virtues. No prior leaders—not the Greeks nor the Romans nor the empires of Europe—had discovered the formula they created. No nations—not even those who tried to imitate their plan—have matched their profound success.

We are enormously privileged to live under the model of free government they designed.

The bottom line, then, is this: Their example is worth our own vigorous investigation and imitation.

Because of the innovation, guts and determination of men like George Washington, Benjamin Franklin, Thomas Jefferson, James Madison, John and Samuel Adams and many others, each of us, as American citizens, have inherited the privilege of selecting those who will lead us every two years. Each generation is free to exercise this right 25-35 times, on average, throughout their lives. We owe it to ourselves, our children, our neighbors our world—and to generations past, present and future—to base our votes on their legacy, the most celebrated and admired foundation for society and government.

Today, we experience many of the same challenges they faced, although in different form. Powerful and insidious threats to our security, our prosperity, our moral standards, even to our rule of law—both internal and external—face this generation as never before. It's encouraging to learn that even these dangers were foreseen and anxiously prepared for by our founders. We are wise to listen to their concerns and heed their warnings.

Fortunately, we have so much of the research, conversations and private thoughts of many of these men and women at our fingertips. They are our dowry, our winning ticket; they are the currency with which we can purchase, for our America and for our world, the freedom, prosperity and happiness they envisioned and sacrificed to establish.

Today, each of us must choose whether we, both as individuals and as a people, are to emulate or ignore them. For our future's sake, we must choose well.

And so I repeat, "You get what you pay for."

PART I
THE EXPERIMENT

CHAPTER 1

AN AMERICAN VISION

Few could have imagined, as the revolution against Britain wound down, what would lie ahead for the toughened, war-weary but eager new nation. It would take brief but anxious periods of chaos, division, class rivalries and outright insurrection before these fledgling states and their leaders would ratify a common federal constitution to define and empower their new government and set the course for following generations of Americans and, indeed, the entire civilized world.

This "American" ideal was unique: It was innovative, yet based in large part on ancient principles. It was brash, yet humble. It was absolute in its declarations yet supple in its allowance for self-correction, if correction was needed. And it was traditional, yet wholly revolutionary.

Above all, it was an experiment in freedom, the result of a decidedly American vision of permanent civil, spiritual and economic independence for all.

Read some of the founders' own thoughts regarding that incredible vision of political freedom and, in particular, of what is required for good government of that freedom.

DAY 1

BENJAMIN FRANKLIN

"The good will of the governed will be starved if not fed by the good deeds of the governors."

Poor Richard's Almanack, 1753

Today Dr. Franklin might write:

Citizens will lose faith in government if their leaders fail to lead them well.

DAY 2

THOMAS JEFFERSON

"The whole art of government consists in the art of being honest."

Essay, Rights of British America, 1774

Today Mr. Jefferson might write:

The only artistry needed to govern well is the art of being open and honest with the people.

DAY 3

PATRICK HENRY

"The liberties of a people never were, nor ever will be, secure, when the transactions of their rulers may be concealed from them."

Remarks to the Virginia Ratifying Convention, June 9, 1788

Today Mr. Henry might say:

A nation's freedoms have never been—and will never be—safe when their government does the peoples' business without transparency.

DAY 4

GEORGE WASHINGTON

"Let prejudices, unreasonable jealousies, and local interest yield to reason and liberality. Let us look to our national character, and to things beyond the present period."

To James Madison, November 5, 1786

Today Mr. Washington might write:

Partisanship, foolish rivalries and local concerns should step aside and let reasonable and open minds take the lead. Let's focus, instead, on the dignity and character of America and on what our shared future can be.

DAY 5

THOMAS JEFFERSON

"It is error, alone, which needs the support of government. Truth can stand on its own. Subject opinion to coercion: whom will you make your inquisitors? Fallible men; men governed by bad passions, by private as well as public reasons. And why subject it to coercion? To produce uniformity. But is uniformity of opinion desireable?"

Notes on the State of Virginia (Query XVII), 1784

Today Mr. Jefferson might write:

Only error needs government to back it up—truth can stand on its own. If we are forced to get approval of our opinions, just who should we ask to approve them? I'll tell you who: Mere men, persuaded by lust and greed and personal, as well as political, agendas. Besides, why would we need their approval? So that everyone wil believe the same thing. But is that what we want?

DAY 6

ALEXANDER HAMILTON

"The true test of a good government is its aptitude and tendency to produce a good administration."

The Federalist, No, 68 (as "Publius"), March 12, 1788

Today Mr. Hamilton might write:

The most reliable evidence of good governing is whether those who govern have the competence and the desire to build an effective government.

DAY 7

THOMAS JEFFERSON

"Great innovations should not be forced on slender majorities."

To General Thaddeus Kosciuszko, May 2, 1808

Today President Jefferson might write:

Government should not impose sweeping changes on an evenly divided nation

DAY 8

THOMAS PAINE

"The forms of government are numerous, and perhaps the simplest is the best."

Essay, Four Letters On Interesting Subjects,* Letter IV 18-24, 1776

(*Authorship disputed)

Day 9

THOMAS PAINE

"When men yield up the exclusive privilege of thinking, the last shadow of liberty quits the horizon."

Common Sense, February 14, 1776

Today Mr. Paine might write:

When people surrender their personal right to think for themselves, the sun has set on their last glimpse of freedom.

Day 10

GEORGE WASHINGTON

"Example, whether it be good or bad, has a powerful influence."

To General William Alexander [aka Lord Stirling), March 5, 1780

CHAPTER 2

A RESOLUTE CONSTITUTION

The American Constitution was purposely constructed to impose reasonable yet resolute limits on all governing bodies, at every level, while providing maximum and enduring freedom to all. Its ideals were based on profound principles applied to all governing officials and maintained by strict and explicit limits of authority and influence.

The founders imagined few civil realms in which the intrusion of government was necessary and genuinely healthy—and they were determined to prevent those given leadership over such realms from undermining the freedoms of the people by overreaching. The result was that both federal and state governments were deliberately designed to block any single branch from breaking its constitutional bonds to unilaterally expand beyond its defined limitations, thereby creating either another monarchy or, worse, a dictatorship.

With exceptional genius, they also built into their constitution sufficient flexibility to leave future generations a simple process for correcting unforeseen failings, without altering its core philosophies or moral foundation. That process cleverly required a high threshold of agreement among the states and their respective citizens to both initiate and approve its amendment.

With few exceptions (many of which occurred during their own lifetimes) their self-created prodigy, the American Constitution, has not needed amendment. It has withstood not only the test of time but assaults of every nature, from within and without, only to be celebrated and emulated by most of the world. And it is why this resolute constitution has remained the unshaken pillar of strength in the middle of a never-ending whirlwind of political and societal upheaval.

You will certainly note that resolve in the words that follow.

DAY 11

ALEXANDER HAMILTON

"A sacred respect for the constitutional law is the vital principle, the sustaining energy of a free government."

Essay in The American Daily Advertiser, 1794

Today Mr. Hamilton might write:

A supreme reverence for Constitutional law is the heart, the engine that nourishes and energizes a free government.

DAY 12

GEORGE WASHINGTON

"[T]he consequences of a lax, or inefficient government, are too obvious to be dwelt on. ...a liberal, and energetic constitution, well guarded and closely watched, to prevent encroachments, might restore us to that degree of respectability and consequence to which we had a fair claim, and the brightest prospect of attaining."

To James Madison, November 5, 1786

Today Mr. Washington might write:

[T]he consequences of a lazy or incompetent government are so obvious it's not worth the time to think about ...An innovative and robust constitution—closely monitored and tightly guarded to prevent power grabs—might help us reclaim that level of respect and influence we once knew and still have high hopes of reaching.

Day 13

CHARLES COTESWORTH PINCKNEY

"When the great work was done and published, I was... struck with amazement. Nothing less than the superintending Hand of Providence, that so miraculously carried us through the war... could have brought it about so complete upon the whole."

Essays on the Constitution, 1792

Today Mr. Pinckney might write:

After this incredible Constitution was finalized and circulated, I sat there, stunned. Only God's active guidance which, miraculously, got us through the war... could have crafted it so perfectly.

Day 14

THOMAS JEFFERSON

"...it is jealousy and not confidence which prescribes limited constitutions to bind down those whom we are obliged to trust with power: that our Constitution has accordingly fixed the limits to which, and no further, our confidence may go... In questions of power, then, let no more be heard of confidence in man, but bind him down from mischief by the chains of the Constitution."

Draft of the Kentucky Resolutions, 1798

Today Vice President Jefferson might write:

It's a reasonable suspicion, not trust, that requires a constitution to harness those to whom we must give power. That's why our Constitution has put strict limits on how far they are to be trusted... So, on questions about power let's not talk any more about trusting in a mere man but about using the Constitution as handcuffs to keep that man from doing mischief.

Day 15

HORATIO BUNCE

"[T]he Constitution, to be worth anything, must be held sacred, and rigidly observed in all its provisions. The man who wields power and misinterprets it is the more dangerous the more honest he is."

[c. 1829], as quoted in "The Life of Colonel David Crockett" by Edward Sylvester Ellis, published 1884

Today Mr. Bunce might say:

For the Constitution to have any value it must be respected as supreme, and every word strictly followed. A man given power to rule who Is mistaken in interpreting its meaning is dangerous; and the more sincere he is the more of a danger he becomes.

Day 16

JOHN DICKINSON

"For who are a free people? Not those over whom government is reasonably and equitably exercised, but those who live under a government so constitutionally checked and controlled that proper provision is made against its otherwise being exercised."

Political Writings, 1767-1768

Today Governor Dickinson might write:

So, how do you define a "free" people? A fair and reasonable government does not create a free people. No, the truly free people are the citizens of a nation under a constitution written in such a way as to allow no flexibility to govern by any other fashion than to uphold freedom.

DAY 17

PATRICK HENRY

"The Constitution is not an instrument for the government to restrain the people, it is an instrument for the people to restrain the government—lest it come to dominate our lives and interests."

Remarks to the Virginia House of Burgesses, Saint John's Church, Richmond, Virginia, March 23, 1775

Today Mr. Henry might say:

The Constitution is not a harness for the government to bind the people. It's really a chain for the people to bind the government to keep it from ultimately controlling every aspect of our lives.

DAY 18

NATHANIEL CHIPMAN

"By giving them the power of avoiding all constitutional enquiry, it places them above a sense of accountability for their conduct. They have it in their power, either in the enacting, the interpretation, or the execution of the laws, to skreen themselves, and every member of their body, from account or punishment."

Sketches of the Principles of Government 120-127, 1793

Today Judge Chipman might write:

If the [executive, legislative and judicial] branches were to be exempt from all constitutional investigations they would no longer be answerable to the people for their actions. Whether enacting law, interpreting law, or executing law, their powers would effectively shield themselves, and all of their staffs, from both accountability and the threat of prosecution.

DAY 19

JOSEPH STORY

"Temporary delusions, prejudices, excitements, and objects have irresistible influence in mere questions of policy. And the policy of one age may ill suit the wishes or the policy of another. The constitution is not subject to such fluctuations. It is to have a fixed, uniform, permanent construction. It should be, so far at least as human infirmity will allow, not dependent upon the passions or parties of particular times, but the same yesterday, to-day, and for ever."

Commentaries on the Constitution, 1833

Today Justice Story might write:

It's very tempting to argue public policy along the lines of short-term fantasies, biases, dreams and goals. And, what one generation may want, another doesn't. But the Constitution isn't that erratic. It should be inflexible, consistent and permanent. Even given the potential for human error, it should be independent of the whims and cravings and cliques each generation brings. [Like God himself] It should be "the same yesterday, today and forever."

DAY 20

THOMAS PAINE

"It is easy to perceive that individuals by agreeing to erect forms of government, for the better security of themselves, must give up some part of their liberty for that purpose; and it is the particular business of a constitution to mark out how much they shall give up."

Essay, Four Letters On Interesting Subjects*, Letter IV 18-24, 1776

Today Mr. Paine might write:

It's easy to see that a group of individuals who agree to form a new government for their own safety have to surrender a portion of their freedom to do so. It's the primary purpose of a constitution to put in writing precisely how much freedom they must surrender.

DAY 21

THOMAS JEFFERSON

"It would reduce the whole instrument to a single phrase, that of instituting a Congress with power to do whatever would be for the good of the United States; and as they would be the sole judges of the good or evil, it would be also a power to do whatever evil they please. Certainly no such universal power was meant to be given them. [The Constitution] was intended to lace them up straightly within the enumerated powers and those without which, as means, these powers could not be carried into effect."

Essay, Opinion on a National Bank, 1791

Today Secretary of State Jefferson might write:

[Allowing Congress to "provide for the general welfare" however they please] would mean, in effect, that one clause would cancel out the rest of the Constitution. If what they deemed "best" was the bottom line, they would have the right to enact whatever corrupt or sinister rules they wanted. It was certainly never intended to give them so much power. On the contrary, the Constitution was designed to put Congress in a straightjacket, restricting them only to those powers specifically listed and the means for meeting their obligations.

DAY 22

GEORGE WASHINGTON

"The basis of our political system is the right of the people to make and to alter their constitutions of government. But the constitution which at any time exists, till changed by an explicit and authentic act of the whole people, is sacredly obligatory upon all. The very idea of the power and the right of the people to establish government presupposes the duty of every individual to obey the established government."

Farewell Address, September 17, 1796

Today President Washington might say:

At the root of our system of government is the peoples' right to design and to change their [federal or state] constitutions. But until it is, in fact, changed—through an intentional and lawful move of all the people—obeying whatever constitution is in force at that time is still the most sacred debt of all Americans. The idea that the people possess the authority and the right to shape their government certainly implies that everyone is obliged to obey it.

DAY 23

JAMES WILSON

"By pursuing the principle of democracy to its true source, we have discovered, that the law is higher than the magistrate, who administers it; that the constitution is higher than both; and that the supreme power, remaining with the people, is higher than all the three."

Lectures on Law: Part 2, Chapter 2, Of the Executive Department, 1791

Today Justice Wilson might write:

If we trace the concept of democracy to its fundamental principles we learn that (1) the law outranks the official who enforces it, that (2) the Constitution outranks both of them and that (3) the citizens, who hold the ultimate power, outrank all three.

DAY 24

THOMAS PAINE

"Next to the forming a good Constitution, is the means of preserving it. If once the legislative power breaks in upon it, the effect will be the same as if a kingly power did it. The Constitution, in either case, will receive its death wound, and 'the outward and visible sign,' or mere form of government only will remain."

Essay, Four Letters On Interesting Subjects*, Letter IV, 18-24, 1776

Today Mr. Paine might write:

Once you form a strong constitution you need to decide how to keep it strong. If Congress should ever overrule our Constitution, it would be as if a conquering power had replaced it with its own. In either scenario, the Constitution would have been murdered and the fading ghost of a [free] government is all that would remain.

DAY 25

HORATIO BUNCE

"The people have delegated to Congress, by the Constitution, the power to do certain things. To do these, it is authorized to collect and pay moneys, and for nothing else. Everything beyond this is usurpation, and a violation of the Constitution."

[c. 1829], as quoted in "The Life of Colonel David Crockett" by Edward Sylvester Ellis, published 1884

Today Mr. Bunce might say:

The people have given Congress the constitutional power to only do specific things. And to do these specific things, the people have given them authority to tax and pay legitimate debts, no more. Anything else is an unlawful seizure—and an assault on the Constitution.

DAY 26

BENJAMIN RUSH

"Where there is no law, there is no liberty; and nothing deserves the name of law but that which is certain and universal in its operation upon all the members of the community."

To David Ramsay, 1788

Today Dr. Rush might write:

Without law you can't have freedom. And the only law worthy of that name has to be firm and applied in the same way to everyone in the community.

CHAPTER 3

ON DIVIDED POWERS

To achieve their lofty aims, the relatively few learned and influential leaders who designed the blueprint for our system of government split the government's rightful powers between three equal branches, each with a mandate to monitor and repair trespasses by the other two. But no single branch can accomplish that alone—each needs another to act in tandem with it to thwart the encroachment of the third.

That simple hypothesis produced a balance that has survived, thrived and been imitated many times over to this day. Nonetheless, it has repeatedly been tested by those of every generation who would exercise their own freedoms in an effort, willingly or not, to undermine those of others—often in the name of "progress."

Even in our times, after a long history of determined defense of the divided powers principle, this fundamental Constitutional feature has been challenged like never before. Some of these challenges have resulted from emergency circumstances, such as the 9/11 assault on America. Most others have been subtle attempts to concentrate more power in the hands of a single branch or, conversely, out of the hands of a rival branch.

This threat remains very real and very fluid. Only a wary and watchful electorate can prevent such silent anarchy. So say those who fought for the privilege of determining which powers those that govern ought to have and how those powers ought to be shared.

Their words may, perhaps ought to, alarm us.

DAY 27

JAMES MADISON

"It will not be denied that power is of an encroaching nature and that it ought to be effectually restrained from passing the limits assigned to it. After discriminating, therefore, in theory, the several classes of power, as they may in their nature be legislative, executive, or judiciary, the next and most difficult task is to provide some practical security for each against the invasion of the others."

The Federalist, No. 48 (as "Publius"), February 1, 1788

Today Mr. Madison might write:

There's no question that power tends, by its nature, to intrude upon others' power so it needs to be kept from overstepping its set boundaries. Once the role of each branch (legislative, executive, judiciary) is defined, the next step is much harder—to devise ways to keep them from invading each other's territory.

DAY 28

GEORGE WASHINGTON

"It is important, likewise, that the habits of thinking in a free country should inspire caution in those intrusted with its administration, to confine themselves within their respective constitutional spheres, avoiding in the exercise of the powers of one department to encroach upon another. The spirit of encroachment tends to consolidate the powers of all the departments in one, and thus to create, whatever the form of government, a real despotism."

Farewell Address, September 17, 1796

Today President Washington might say:

And it's important, also, to recognize that the way free people cherish their freedom should remind those trusted to govern them to use extreme caution and stay only within the confines of their Constitutional authority so they don't hijack the powers given to another branch while exercising their own. Such intrusion leads to centralizing the powers of all branches into a single branch— forging a certain dictatorship no matter which form of government they claim.

DAY 29

JOHN ADAMS

"The essence of a free government consists in an effectual control of rivalries. The executive and the legislative powers are natural rivals; and if each has not an effectual control over the other, the weaker will ever be the lamb in the paws of the wolf."

Discourses on Davila, Number 8, 1790

Today Vice President Adams might write:

Successfully managing rivalries is central to efficiently managing a free government. Since the executive and legislative branches are natural competitors, if either branch can't hold off the other, the weaker one will succumb like a lamb in the grasp of the wolf.

DAY 30

JAMES MADISON

"An elective despotism was not the government we fought for; but one in which the powers of government should be so divided and balanced among the several bodies of magistracy as that no one could transcend their legal limits without being effectually checked and restrained by the others."

The Federalist, No. 58 (as "Publius"), February 20, 1788

Today Mr. Madison might write:

We didn't fight just to end up with an elected tyranny. We fought to build a government that would divide the power, balancing it between each of several bodies of officials in such a way that none of them could cross their constitutional boundaries without being successfully blocked and turned back by the others.

DAY 31

NATHANIEL CHIPMAN

"The members of the legislature, cannot, from the nature of their functions, be amenable, in their legislative character, to any tribunal, but that of public sentiment. The case is different with the members of the executive and judiciary. They may, with propriety, be subjected to trial, for a violation of their trust, at the bar of a constitutional tribunal."

Sketches of the Principles of Government 120-127, 1793

Today Judge Chipman might write:

Because of their role as lawmakers, members of Congress cannot be held accountable to any court but that of the voters. It's a different matter for the executive and judicial branches. Members of these branches can rightly be made to stand trial before a constitutional tribunal for violating the public trust.

DAY 32

JOHN BARNARD

"For one person alone to have the government of a people in his hands, would be too great a temptation. It tends to excite and draw forth the pride of man, to make him insufferably haughty; it gives him too much liberty to exert his corruptions and it encourages him to become a tyrant and an oppressor, to dispense with laws and break the most solemn oaths."

The Presence of Great God in the Assembly of Political Rulers, 1746

Today Rev. Barnard might say:

It would be too tempting for a single individual to hold the people's government in his hands alone. That much power would likely bring out the worst in a person and make him so arrogant he would become unbearable. It would give him too much freedom to impose corruption and provoke him to become a bully and a tyrant, abandoning the rule of law and cancelling long-time promises.

DAY 33

JAMES WILSON

"The person at the head of the executive department had authority, not to make, or alter, or dispense with the laws, but to execute and act the laws, which were established: and against this power there was no rising up, so long as it gadded not, like an unfeathered arrow, at random... On the whole, he was no

other than a primum mobile set in a regular motion by laws,
which were established by the whole body of the nation."

Lectures on Law: Of the Executive Department, 1791

Today Justice Wilson might write:

*The president must make sure that the laws are closely enforced.
[Based on the Saxon "first executive" model,] the president has no
authority to make, change or ignore laws; he can only enforce
those laws that are on the books... He cannot refuse to carry out
laws as long as they were not passed in a haphazard manner...
Basically, [executive authority] was merely a planet set in motion
by the laws enacted by the peoples' representatives.*

DAY 34

NATHANIEL CHIPMAN

"The executive is, in all cases, the ultimately efficient power. It
is, therefore, very necessary, that the executive should be
limited, with as much precision, as the nature of the power will
permit, and the acts of all its ministers, rendered as
conspicuous, as may possibly be, or, at least, of easy
investigation, and the ministers themselves made amenable to
the ordinary, or constitutional tribunals, for every abuse."

Sketches of the Principles of Government 120-127, 1793

Today Judge Chipman might write:

*The simplest and most efficient way [to govern] would be to hand
all power over to one executive. For that reason, limitations
placed on the president must be as specific as the nature of that
job allows. In addition, all moves by his appointees should be
transparent and subject to investigation and the appointees
themselves must submit to either a court of law or a
constitutional trial for each abuse of their authority.*

Day 35

ALEXANDER HAMILTON

"This balance between the national and state governments ought to be dwelt on with peculiar attention, as it is of the utmost importance. It forms a double security to the people. If one encroaches on their rights they will find a powerful protection in the other. Indeed, they will both be prevented from overpassing their constitutional limits by a certain rivalship, which will ever subsist between them."

Remarks to the New York Ratifying Convention, 1788

Today Mr. Hamilton might say:

Since it is critically important, we should pay special attention to balancing the roles of the federal and state governments. The proper balance gives the people twice the security. If one intrudes on their freedom, the other will forcefully protect them. In fact, both powers will then be kept in check from expanding their constitutional borders by the constant tension that will inevitably exist between them.

Day 36

THOMAS JEFFERSON

"I consider the foundation of the Constitution as laid on this ground that 'all powers not delegated to the United States, by the Constitution, nor prohibited by it to the states, are reserved to the states or to the people.' To take a single step beyond the boundaries thus specially drawn around the powers of Congress, is to take possession of a boundless field of power, not longer susceptible of any definition."

To George Washington, on the Constitutionality of the Bank of the United States, 1791

Today Secretary of State Jefferson might write:

My view is that the heart and soul of our Constitution fundamentally gives all power not explicitly assigned to the federal government, nor explicitly withheld from the states, either to states or to their citizens. To cross over those lines specifically drawn around Congress in any way is to claim the right to unlimited and uncontrollable powers.

DAY 37

JAMES MADISON

"The powers delegated by the proposed Constitution to the federal government are few and defined. Those which are to remain in the state governments are numerous and indefinite."

Federalist Papers, No. 45 (as "Publius"), January 26, 1788

Today Justice Story might write:

The proposed Constitution doesn't give much power to the federal government -- and makes very clear those it does give. On the other hand, the powers given to state governments are plentiful and purposely vague.

DAY 38

JOSEPH STORY

"The constitution of the United States is to receive a reasonable interpretation of its language, and its powers, keeping in view the objects and purposes, for which those powers were conferred. By a reasonable interpretation, we mean, that in case the words are susceptible of two different senses, the one strict, the other more enlarged, that should be adopted, which is most consonant with the apparent objects and intent of the Constitution."

Commentaries on the Constitution, 1833

Today Justice Story might write:

The language used in the U.S. Constitution should be interpreted reasonably, keeping in mind the intended goals and objectives for assigning powers in the way they did. In other words, when words have multiple meanings, one narrow and another broad, the meaning that is most consistent with the clear intentions of its framers is the one that should be applied.

DAY 39

JAMES MADISON

"As the courts are generally the last in making the decision, it results to them, by refusing or not refusing to execute a law, to stamp it with its final character. This makes the Judiciary department paramount in fact to the Legislature, which was never intended and can never be proper."

To John Brown of Kentucky, Remarks on Jefferson's "Draft of a Constitution for Virginia," October 15, 1788

Today Mr. Madison might write:

Since arguments typically end up in a court of law, it's the judge who, in deciding whether or not to enforce the law, has the final say. In effect, that makes the judiciary branch more powerful than the legislative, which was never the intent of the framers. Under no circumstances will such a practice ever be acceptable.

DAY 40

GEORGE WASHINGTON

"In all our deliberations on this subject we kept steadily in our view, that which appears to us the greatest interest of every true American, the consolidation of our union, in which is involved our prosperity, felicity, safety, perhaps our national existence."

Letter [to the States] Transmitting the Proposed Constitution from the Federal Convention to the Confederation Congress," September 17, 1787

Today Mr. Washington might write:

In all of our discussions about [balancing state and federal powers] we stayed focused on what we believe to be the most important benefit for all true Americans—the unifying of our nation—which will determine our wealth, happiness, security and even, perhaps, our national survival.

DAY 41

JOHN QUINCY ADAMS

"To respect the rights of the state governments is the inviolable duty of that of the union; the government of every State will feel its own obligation to respect and preserve the rights of the whole."

Inaugural Address, March 4, 1825

Today President Adams might say:

The federal government must, without exception, respect the rights of state governments. All state governments will, likewise, feel obliged to respect and defend the rights of both.

DAY 42

JAMES MADISON

"But ambitious encroachments of the federal government on the authority of the state governments would not excite the opposition of a single state, or of a few states only. They would be signals of general alarm... But what degree of madness could ever drive the federal government to such an extremity."

The Federalist, No. 46 (as "Publius"), January 29, 1788

Today Mr. Madison might write:

However, aggressive interference by the federal government into state authority wouldn't motivate resistance from just one state or even from a few. No, it would rally all of them to unite and resist... But what kind of extreme insanity could ever drive the federal government to take such radical action?

CHAPTER 4

A NOBLE PRESIDENCY

Constitutional Convention delegate Pierce Butler wrote of the struggle to define the American presidency that he did not believe the powers of the presidency "would have been so great had not many of the members cast their eyes towards General Washington as President and shaped their ideas of the powers to be given to a president by their opinions of his virtue."

The founding fathers saw their beloved general and leader as the model of all they wanted the American presidency to embody. Noble, principled, unbiased, brave, proud and competent—these were just some of the qualities that set him above his peers. And it was those peers who defined the most important office in the land with him in mind.

There have been no equals among the many generations that have followed Washington's presidency. Nor can we honestly expect them. But we ought to expect that our presidents emulate his integrity and his unfailing commitment to govern all Americans thoughtfully and with a profound and humble wisdom.

Nobility may be an overlooked and "old fashioned" characteristic in these times but it is still worth seeking in those who would lead us. Just ask those who did so first.

JOSEPH STORY

"A feeble executive implies a feeble execution of the government. A feeble execution is but another phrase for a bad execution; and a government ill executed, whatever may be its theory, must, in practice, be a bad government."

Commentaries on the Constitution, 1833

Today Justice Story might write:

A weak president is a sign of a weak government. Weakness is just a synonym for incompetence. And an incompetent government, no matter what the excuse, is a bad government, period.

DAY 44

THOMAS JEFFERSON

"A free people [claim] their rights as derived from the laws of nature, and not as the gift of their chief magistrate."

Essay, Rights of British America, 1774

Today Mr. Jefferson might write:

The rights of a free people are given by nature's law, not as a gift from the head of their government.

DAY 45

GEORGE WASHINGTON

"The executive branch of this government never has, nor will suffer, while I preside, any improper conduct of its officers to escape with impunity."

To Gouverneur Morris, December 22, 1795

Today President Washington might write:

My administration never has, and never will, allow any inappropriate conduct by my appointees to be exempt from due justice—not while I am president.

DAY 46

THOMAS JEFFERSON

"An honest man can feel no pleasure in the exercise of power over his fellow citizens."

To John Melish, 1813

DAY 47

CONSTITUTIONAL CONVENTION DELEGATES

"...he shall take Care that the Laws be faithfully executed..."

Article 2, Section 3 of the United States Constitution

Today the Convention delegates might conclude that:

[The president] shall make sure that the laws are enforced as they were written...

DAY 48

GEORGE WASHINGTON

"I give my signature to many bills with which my judgment is at variance.... From the nature of the Constitution, I must approve all parts of a bill, or reject it in total. To do the latter can only be justified upon the clear and obvious grounds of propriety; and I never had such confidence in my own faculty of judging as to be over tenacious of the opinions I may have imbibed in doubtful cases."

To Edmund Pendleton, September 23, 1793

Today President Washington might write:

I sign a lot of bills that I disagree with. ...Our Constitution demands that I either approve or reject the whole bill. A rejection can only be justified when it's clearly and obviously right to do so. I've never thought so highly of my own judgment to stubbornly impose the conclusions I might have reached on debatable issues.

DAY 49

TENCH COXE

"In America, as the president is to be one of the people at the end of his short term, so will he and his fellow citizens remember that he was originally one of the people and that he is created by their breath."

Pamphlet, An Examination of the Constitution for the United States of America..., #1 (under the pseudonym, "An American Citizen")

Today Mr. Coxe might write:

In America, since the president will become just another ordinary citizen when his brief term is up, he and his fellow citizens will recall that he had been one of them before—and that it was these same people that had breathed life into his presidency.

Day 50

JAMES MADISON

"I think it absolutely necessary that the President should have the power of removing [his subordinates] from office; it makes him, in a peculiar manner, responsible for their conduct and subjects him to impeachment himself."

Remarks in the House of Representatives, May 19, 1789

Today Congressman Madison might say:

In my opinion, the president must be given the authority to fire his subordinates. It may seem strange, but having such authority keeps him accountable for their performance and puts his own job on the line.

Day 51

JAMES WILSON

"Happy the nation, in which pardons will be considered as dangerous! Clemency is a virtue which belongs to the legislator, and not to the executor of the laws; a virtue, which should shine in the code, and not in private judgment."

Lectures on Law: Part 2, Chapter 2, Of the Executive Department, 1791

Today Justice Wilson might write:

The nation that views pardons as dangerous is better off. Leniency is a privilege that belongs to those who make the law, not the one who enforces the law. But such an exemption, if it should be offered at all, should be rooted in the legal code, not as the result of a conclusion reached in the privacy of one man's personal opinion.

TENCH COXE

"In all great cases affecting the national interests or safety, his modified and restrained power must give way to the sense of two-thirds of the legislature. In fact it amounts to no more, than a serious duty imposed upon him to request both houses to re-consider any matter on which he entertains doubts or feels apprehensions; and here the people have a strong hold upon him from his sole and personal responsibility."

Pamphlet, An Examination of the Constitution for the United States of America..., #1 (under the pseudonym, "An American Citizen")

Today Mr. Coxe might write:

Whenever the interests or safety of the nation are affected, the limited authority [of the president, as compared to the king] must yield to the decision of two-thirds of the Congress. The fact is, taking seriously the responsibility given only to him, all he can do is ask both houses to take another look at any decision he finds doubtful or troubling. Whenever this happens, he must remember that he, alone, has been given the sole and personal responsibility for how the matter affects all of the people.

GEORGE WASHINGTON

"Integrity and firmness are all I can promise. These, though the voyage be long or short, shall never forsake me, although I may be deserted by all men; for all of the consolations which are to be derived from these, under any circumstances, the world cannot deprive me."

To General Henry Knox, April 1, 1789

Today President-Elect Washington might write:

I can only promise to be honest and firm. Whether my journey [in office] is short or long, these qualities will never leave me even if everyone deserts me. And the world can never, in any circumstance, take away the comfort I gain from them.

CHAPTER 5

A RESPECTED CONGRESS

From an anomalous and momentary high of 84% in October 2001, Congressional approval ratings began a headlong plunge, reaching an historic low of 9% in November of 2013. This ongoing trend is truly abysmal. Americans have lost confidence in their representatives; much of the electorate finds them irrelevant, incompetent and highly partisan.

The founders, of course, envisioned a much different scenario. The constitutional system of leadership they devised was intended to create a prototype for regional participation in the federal government that would generate the esteem, respect and trust of the American voters which would, in turn, ensure both unity and progress for the new nation.

Still, those hopes were rightly tempered by a healthy distrust of the kinds of people who may be drawn by the power and appeal of the office. Influential charlatans and charismatic charmers could clearly invalidate the promise of their plan. Add to the mix their fears of an apathetic or easily manipulated electorate and you end up with a 9% approval rating.

These fears have proven accurate throughout the history of the democratic republic form of government.

Read their warnings to future generations, including—perhaps especially—to ours.

DAY 54

GEORGE MASON

"How easy it is to persuade men to sign anything by which they can't be affected!"

To Zachariah Johnston, 1791

Today Mr. mason might say:

It's so easy to get men to sign something when it won't have any impact on their own lives!

DAY 55

DAVID CROCKETT

"I would rather be politically dead than hypocritically immortalized."

Speech in the US House of Representatives, Feburary 14, 1831

Today Congressman Crockett might say:

I would rather forfeit my political career than be remembered forever as a hypocrite.

Day 56

JAMES MADISON

"It will be of little avail to the people, that the laws are made by men of their own choice, if the laws be so voluminous that they cannot be read, or so incoherent that they cannot be understood; if they be repealed or revised before they are promulgated, or undergo such incessant changes that no man, who knows what the law is to-day, can guess what it will be to-morrow. Law is defined to be a rule of action; but how can that be a rule, which is little known, and less fixed?"

The Federalist, No. 62 (as "Publius"), Feburary 27, 1788

Today Mr. Madison might write:

It doesn't help the people that the laws are made by men they elected if the laws they make are so lengthy they can't be read, so confusing they can't be understood, are withdrawn or amended before they're published or are changed so much and so often that no one who knows what the law demands today can even imagine what it might demand tomorrow. Law is defined as "a rule governing action" but how can it be a rule when no one knows what the rule is because it's constantly changing?

Day 57

THOMAS JEFFERSON

"Experience having long taught me the reasonableness of mutual sacrifices of opinion among those who are to act together for any common object, and the practicality of doing what good we can; when we cannot do all we would wish."

To John Randolph, 1803

Today President Jefferson might write:

Life taught me long ago that compromise may be useful for those who need to work together to realize a common goal; it makes sense to achieve whatever good we can, even if we can't get all the good that we want.

DAY 58

JAMES WILSON

"Let the laws be clear and simple: let the entire force of the nation be united in their defence: let them, and them only, be feared. The fear of the laws is salutary: but the fear of man is a fruitful and a fatal source of crimes."

Lectures on Law: Part 2, Chapter 2, Of the Executive Department, 1791

Today Justice Wilson might write:

Make laws that are clear and simple and the might of all the people will unite to protect them. Only laws are to be feared. It's helpful to fear laws but fearing men is a fertile and deadly cause of crime.

DAY 59

THOMAS JEFFERSON

"Laws are made for men of ordinary understanding and should, therefore, be construed by the ordinary rules of common sense. Their meaning is not to be sought for in metaphysical subtleties which may make anything mean everything or nothing at pleasure."

To William Johnson, 1823

Today Mr. Jefferson might write:

Laws are made to be understood by the average person, so they should follow basic rules of common sense. They can't be so broad that they cover virtually everything or so narrow that they cover virtually nothing; this doesn't need to be as complicated as abstract philosophy.

DAY 60

DAVID CROCKETT

"I am no man's man. I bark at no man's bid. I will never come and go, and fetch and carry, at the whistle of the great man in the white house, no matter who he is. And if this petty, un-patriotic scuffling for men, and forgetting principles, goes on, it will be the overthrow of this one happy nation, and the blood and toil of our ancestors will have been expended in vain."

Speech, [c. 1831-4], "An Account of Col. Crockett's Tour to the North and Down East" (Autobiographical, published in 1834)

Today Congressman Crockett might say:

I'm no one's stooge. I don't jump when any man calls. I will never do tricks when the president whistles, no matter who the president is. And if this trivial, un-American and unhealthy competition for votes—while compromising on principle—continues, this peaceful nation, and the blood and sweat of our ancestors, will have been pointless.

DAY 61

HORATIO BUNCE

"In the first place, the government ought to have in the Treasury no more than enough for its legitimate purposes... So you see, Colonel, you have violated the Constitution in what I consider a vital point. It is a precedent fraught with danger to the country, for when Congress once begins to stretch its power beyond the limits of the Constitution, there is no limit to it, and no security for the people."

[c. 1832] To David Crockett, quoted in "The Life of Colonel David Crockett" by Edward Sylvester Ellis, published 1884

Today Mr. Bunce might say:

First of all, the government should not have more In the bank than it needs to meet its duties... So you can see, Colonel, that you've violated what I think is a key theme of the Constitution. This sets a very dangerous precedent for our nation; when Congress starts extending its powers beyond what the Constitution allows there's nothing to prevent their excess and no safety net for the citizens.

DAY 62

THOMAS JEFFERSON

"Were it made a question, whether no law, as among the savage Americans, or too much law, as among the civilized Europeans, submits man to the greatest evil, one who has seen both conditions of existence would pronounce it to be the last; and that the sheep are happier of themselves, than under care of the wolves."

Notes on Virginia Q.XI, 1782

Today Mr. Jefferson might write:

If you were to ask me which is worse to live under, no set laws like Native Americans or too many laws like Europeans, I'd say that anyone who has observed them both would answer "under too many laws"—given that sheep would rather be left to care for themselves than to be cared for by wolves.

DAY 63

JOHN ADAMS

"When legislature is corrupted, the people are undone."
A Defense of the Constitutions of Government, vol 1, 1787

Today Mr. Adams might write:

When Congress becomes corrupt the peoples' freedom is lost.

DAY 64

JOHN MARSHALL

"[S]hould Congress, under the pretext of executing its powers, pass laws for the accomplishment of objects not entrusted to the government, such [acts are] not the law of the land."
McCulloch v. Maryland, 1819

Today Chief Justice Marshall might rule that:

Any "laws" Congress passes (claiming to be exercising its authority) that deal with areas outside the government's limited boundaries aren't really laws.

DAY 65

ALEXANDER HAMILTON

"The law… dictated by God Himself is, of course, superior in obligation to any other. It is binding over all the globe, in all countries, and at all times. No human laws are of any validity if contrary to this."

Essay, The Farmer Refuted, February 23, 1775

Today Mr. Hamilton might write:

It's obvious that the Law decreed by God, Himself, is to be obeyed above all other laws. This law is binding across the globe, in all nations and at all times. Any human law that contradicts this law is illegitimate.

DAY 66

EDMUND RANDOLPH

"The Senate will be more likely to corrupt than the House of Representatives, and should therefore have less to do with money matters."

Remarks to the Consitutional Congress, 1787

Today Governor Randolph might say:

It's more likely that the Senate could be corrupted than the House of Representatives. So the Senate should have less say on economic policy.

DAY 67

DAVID CROCKETT

"I am now here in Congress... I am at liberty to vote as my conscience and judgment dictates to be right, without the yoke of any party on me, or the driver at my heels, with his whip in hand, commanding me to ge-wo-haw, just at his pleasure. Look at my arms, you will find no party hand-cuff on them!"

To an unknown correspondent, January 28, 1834

Today Congressman Crockett might write:

So, here I am in Congress... I can vote however my conscience and judgment tell me is right. I'm the workhorse for no party; there's no plowman pushing me along, whip in hand, hollering "giddyup" at me whenever he pleases. Look at my wrists—you won't see any party's handcuffs on them!

CHAPTER 6

A Prudent Judiciary

Our American Constitution is unique, in part because it has at its foundation an unwavering devotion to the rule of law. No tyrant or faction can legitimately discard, undermine or override the rule of law with impunity; that is, unless all three branches and the American voters themselves—whether in good conscience or due to indifference and ignorance—approve of such subversion.

This was—and is—the basis for our legal system and the role assigned to the judicial branch of government at all levels. From the part-time rural magistrate to the Chief Justice of the U.S. Supreme Court, judges are expected to regard the relevant law and jurisdictional precedent as sacrosanct, not to be ignored except, on very rare occasion and under the most threatening and immediate circumstances. Neither personal political views nor public enthusiasm for or against a matter before the court is within the discretion of that court; the rule of law, alone, must prevail.

Our founding patriarchs knew well the dangers and temptations of partisan, patronized or advocacy judgments; these matters—even in the most nominal cases—would deprive citizens of their constitutional and moral rights and could ultimately lead to anarchy or tyranny.

Their words reflect such warnings and are as relevant today as when they were expressed centuries ago. We are wise to heed them as we consider candidates for judgeships or for elected officers given power, by state or federal constitutions, to appoint them.

Day 68

THOMAS JEFFERSON

"The Constitution is a mere thing of wax in the hands of the judiciary which they may twist and shape into any form they please."

To Judge Spencer Roane, September 6, 1819

Day 69

JOHN MARSHALL

"Judicial power is never exercised for the purpose of giving effect to the will of the judge; always for the purpose of giving effect to the will of the legislature or, in other words, to the will of the Law."

Osborn vs. Bank of the United States, 1824

Today Chief Justice Marshall might rule that:

The power of the bench must never be used to lend credibility to the judge's wish but always to add authority to the wish of Congress... or, in other words, to the wish of the legislation itself.

Day 70

EDMUND BURKE

"It is the function of a judge not to make but to declare the law, according to the golden mete-wand of the law and not by the crooked cord of discretion."

Preface to Brissot's Address, 1794

Today Mr. Burke might write:

It's a judge's job to declare the applicable law, not to create one. He must use the straight edge of the law, only, as his measuring stick, not the twisted line of his own preference.

DAY 71

JAMES WILSON

The first and governing maxim in the interpretation of a statute is to discover the meaning of those who made it."

Of the Study of Law in the United States, 1790

Today Justice Wilson might write:

The primary principle to apply when interpreting a law is to determine what was meant by those who made the law."

DAY 72

THOMAS JEFFERSON

"On every question of construction, carry yourselves back to the time when the Constitution was adopted, recollect the spirit manifested in the debates, and instead of trying what meaning may be squeezed out of the text, or invented against it, conform to the probable one in which it was passed."

To Supreme Court Justice William Johnson, June 12, 1823

Today Mr. Jefferson might write:

To decide the meaning of the Constitution, look at what was expressed or implied in the debates when it was adopted. Then, instead of guessing what they probably meant or making something up that's obviously contrary to their real intent, just stick to the meaning that was most likely what they meant when they passed it.

DAY 73

JAMES MADISON

"No man is allowed to be a judge in his own cause, because his interest would certainly bias his judgment, and, not improbably, corrupt his integrity."

The Federalist, No. 10 (as "Publius"), November 22, 1787

Today Mr. Madison might write:

[The law] allows no one to judge his own case. His personal stake in the outcome would surely cloud his judgment and probably corrupt his character.

DAY 74

JOHN MARSHALL

"[I]t is not on slight implication and vague conjecture that the legislature is to be pronounced to have transcended its powers and its acts to be considered as void. The opposition between the Constitution and the law should be such that the judge feels a clear and strong conviction of their incompatibilty with each other."

Fletcher vs. Peck, 1810

Today Chief Justice Marshall might rule that:

A court ruling declaring that Congress has overstepped its boundaries—and, therefore, its legislation is null and void—should not be based on vague guesswork and legal trivia. The judge must have an unmistakable and absolute conviction that the legislation contradicts the Constitution.

DAY 75

THOMAS JEFFERSON

"Our judges are as honest as other men and not more so. They have, with others, the same passions for party, for power, and the privilege of their corps."

To W. C. Jarvis, 1820

Today Mr. Jefferson might write:

American judges are no more and no less honest than any other Americans. Just like everyone else, they crave partisanship, power and the perks of office.

PART II
THE PURSUIT

CHAPTER 7

AN AMERICAN DIGNITY

Terror to their north, poverty to their south, mystery to their west and tyranny to their east; all directions held threats to the kind of lives our ancestors, or theirs, had sought. But none of these dangers could deter the founders from pursuing their goal of forging a new, "American," dignity out of the remnants of a past determined by, and for, the crown and the Parliament.

They would not allow that situation to continue unchallenged. This was their time to right longstanding and inherited wrongs. Even some in Parliament, like Edmund Burke, stood with the gritty colonials in seeking a new kind of political liberty.

Read of their courage and firm persistence in forming a new society on ancient principles, one that would be able to ensure freedom and dignity for all.

Day 76

EDMUND BURKE

"There is a boundary to men's passions when they act from feeling; none when they are under the influence of imagination."

An Appeal from the New to the Old Whigs, 1791

Today Mr. Burke might write:

There's a limit to how far people might go when they're protesting against the government, but you can't effectively restrain people under the spell of a new theory of governing.

Day 77

PATRICK HENRY

"For my part, whatever anguish of spirit it may cost, I am willing to know the whole truth; to know the worst, and to provide for it."

Remarks to the Virginia House of Burgesses, Saint John's Church, Richmond, Virginia, March 23, 1775

Day 78

ALEXANDER HAMILTON

"The fundamental source of all your errors, sophisms and false reasonings is a total ignorance of the natural rights of mankind. Were you once to become acquainted with these, you could never entertain a thought, that all men are not, by nature, entitled to a parity of privileges. You would be convinced, that natural liberty is a gift of the beneficent Creator to the whole human race, and that civil liberty is founded in that; and cannot be wrested from any people, without the most manifest violation of justice."

Essay, The Farmer Refuted, February 23, 1775

Today Mr. Hamilton might write:

The underlying cause of all of your mistakes, nonsense and bad logic is that you are totally ignorant of man's natural rights. If you ever studied them you wouldn't buy the notion that people aren't naturally entitled to equal rights. You would be convinced that freedom, like nature itself, is given to all people by a generous Creator. You'd recognize that this divine gift is, in fact, the very foundation of civil freedom and that it is the worst abuse of justice to steal this freedom from any person.

DAY 79

THOMAS PAINE

"I love the man that can smile in trouble, that can gather strength from distress, and grow brave by reflection. 'Tis the business of little minds to shrink; but he whose heart is firm, and whose conscience approves his conduct, will pursue his principles unto death."

Essay, The American Crisis, No. 1, 1776

Today Mr. Paine might write:

I love the person who can laugh at trouble, gain strength in misery and discover courage in careful contemplation. Small minds can only get smaller, but a determined man with a clear conscience will follow his beliefs until he dies.

JOHN ADAMS

"But in demonstrating by our conduct that we do not fear war in the necessary protection of our rights and honor we shall give no room to infer that we abandon the desire of peace. "

Second Annual Address to Congress, December 8, 1798

Today President Adams might say:

But by acting courageously, showing that we will not run from war if that's all that will protect our rights and promote our honor as [Americans], we must also make it clear that we will not turn our backs on a reasonable peace.

BENJAMIN FRANKLIN

"Without steadiness and perseverance no virtue can long subsist, and however honest and well-meaning a man's principles may be the want of this is sufficient to render them ineffectual and useless to himself or others."

Essay, On Constancy, published in The Pennsylvania Gazette, April 4, 1734

Today Dr. Franklin might write:

Integrity won't survive long without consistency and sacrifice. No matter how sincere a man's ideals may be, his lack of these qualities is all it takes to make those ideals meaningless. That man is of no use to himself or to others.

DAY 82

GEORGE MASON

"That no free government, or the blessings of liberty, can be preserved to any people but by a firm adherence to justice, moderation, temperance, frugality and virtue and by frequent recurrence to fundamental principles."

Virginia Declaration of Rights, June 12, 1776

Today Mr. Mason might write:

Only an unwavering commitment to the consistent practice of man's core values—fairness, balance, self-control, economic restraint and dignity—can guarantee the survival of an open government and the blessings of freedom.

DAY 83

JOHN ADAMS

"Children should be educated and instructed in the principles of freedom."

Published in The Works of John Adams, vol VI, compiled by Charles Francis Adams, 1856

DAY 84

SAMUEL WEST

"An enemy to good government is an enemy not only to his country, but to all mankind... Hence we find that wise and good men, of all nations and religions, have ever inculcated subjection to good government, and have borne their testimony against the licentious disturbers of the public peace."

Election Sermon; The True Principles of Government, May 29, 1776

Today Reverend West might say:

The enemy of good governance is not just an enemy of his country but of all of humanity. Knowing this, we recognize that good and wise men of all nations and faiths have always urged compliance with good government—and confront those who brazenly disrupt public peace.

DAY 85

THOMAS PAINE

"If there must be trouble, let it be in my day, that my child may have peace."

Essay, The American Crisis, No. 1, 1776

DAY 86

DANIEL WEBSTER

"The dignity of history consists in reciting events with truth and accuracy, and in presenting human agents and their actions in an interesting and instructive form. The first element in history, therefore, is truthfulness; and this truthfulness must be displayed in a concrete form."

Speech, The Dignity and Importance of History (before the Historical Society of New York), February 23, 1852

Today Secretary of State Webster might say:

The trick to passing on the majesty of history is to reconstruct events truly and accurately and explain the feats of historical figures with clarity and appeal. So, the essential key to unveiling history is truth, and to present truth in a coherent manner.

DAY 87

JOHN ADAMS

"A constitution founded on these principles introduces knowledge among the people, and inspires them with a conscious dignity becoming freemen; a general emulation takes place, which causes good humor, sociability, good manners, and good morals to be general. That elevation of sentiment inspired by such a government, makes the common people brave and enterprising. That ambition which is inspired by it makes them sober, industrious, and frugal."

To Richard Henry Lee, draft of an essay, "Thoughts on Government: Applicable to the Present State of the American Colonies," November 15, 1775

Today Mr. Adams might write:

Such a constitution, based on these principles [i.e., divided powers and term limits], inspires learning and gives a sense of dignity only a free people can know. That confidence will breed communities in which congeniality, civility, friendliness and high moral standards are the rule. When government inspires an increase in these qualities, the people become bold and resourceful. And that enthusiasm encourages a thoughtful, productive and thrifty outlook.

DAY 88

GEORGE WASHINGTON

"The value of liberty was thus enhanced in our estimation by the difficulty of its attainment, and the worth of characters appreciated by the trial of adversity."

Letter to the people of South Carolina, 1790

Today President Washington might write:

Freedom grew even more meaningful to us because the battle to win it was so long and painful and the character of all who suffered was strengthened as a result.

DAY 89

THOMAS PAINE

"Those who expect to reap the blessings of freedom, must, like men, undergo the fatigues of supporting it."

Essay, The American Crisis, No. 4, 1777

Today Mr. Paine might write:

If you expect to taste the blessings of freedom, you must be ready to stand for it no matter how tired or frustrated you may get.

CHAPTER 8

AN AMERICAN PATRIOTISM

The Merriam-Webster dictionary defines *patriot* as "a person who vigorously supports their country and is prepared to defend it against enemies or detractors." It hasn't been that long since patriots were generally portrayed as honorable heroes, respected and worthy of imitation.

But, today's patriot is often ridiculed as an extremist, a zealous phony, an amusing caricature. Sadly, throughout our history, some have used that term to incite fools to rally behind their schemes or to invoke a false sense of nationalism for their own dubious causes.

But to our founders, "patriot," was among the most cherished titles a man or woman could receive; a sign of respect and decency, of character and courage under fire.

The true American patriot was held in the highest esteem by those whom we now hold in the highest esteem. Patriots fought, and won, independence from Britain, not merely for themselves but for those who, for various reasons, didn't fight. Patriots inspired and stirred their neighbors to seek a new kind of freedom, a freedom that was worth a war to claim for themselves and their families yet to come.

Read of their frustration with those who brought indignation on that name and of their awe for those whose dignity had earned it.

JONATHAN MAYHEW

"The very name of patriotism is indeed become a jest with some men; which would be much stranger than it is, had not so many others made a jest of the thing, serving their own base and wicked ends, under the pretext and colour of it. But there will be hypocrites in politicks, as well as in religion. Nor ought so sacred a name to fall into contempt, however it may have been prostituted & profaned, to varnish over crimes.

Election sermon, 1754

Today Reverend Mayhew might say:

Patriotism has been given a bad name, even becoming a joke to some. That used to be rare, but now so many con men deliberately misuse the term to ridicule and intimidate— shamefully playing to their crowd—that it's becoming commonplace. Politics will always have its fair share of hypocrites (just like religion), but we must never let the proud title of "patriot" become the object of contempt just because frauds and crooks have sometimes prostituted and cheapened that name by hiding behind it to disguise their crimes.

DAY 91

BENJAMIN RUSH

"Patriotism is as much a virtue as justice and is as necessary for the support of societies as natural affection [is] in the support of families."

Untitled Essay, 1783

Day 92

THOMAS PAINE

"These are the times that try men's souls. The summer soldier and the sunshine patriot will, in this crisis, shrink from the services of their country but he that stands it NOW deserves the love and thanks of man and woman."

Essay, The American Crisis, No. 1, 1776

Today Mr. Paine might write:

Times like these show what men are really made of. Like the soldier who fights only in good weather or the so-called "patriot" who supports his country only when things go well, some will cringe when asked to serve their country in such times. But those that stand tall TODAY earn the love and gratitude of their neighbors.

Day 93

GEORGE WASHINGTON

"We should never despair, our situation before has been unpromising and has changed for the better, so I trust, it will again. If new difficulties arise, we must only put forth new exertions and proportion our efforts to the exigency of the times."

To Philip Schuyler, July 15, 1777

Today General Washington might write:

We can't give in! Our situation has been discouraging before but has improved—I am confident it will again. And if more troubles come, we'll just have to work harder and strive to meet the demands of the times.

Day 94

JOHN PAUL JONES

"An honorable peace is and always was my first wish! I can take no delight in the effusion of human blood; but if this war should continue, I wish to have the most active part in it."

To Gouverneur Morris, September 2, 1782

Today Captain Jones might write:

My preference has been, and will remain, an honorable peace. I don't care to see any more streams of blood, but if this fight must continue to be fought, I want to be there on the front lines.

Day 95

THOMAS PAINE

"A little matter will move a party, but it must be something great that moves a nation."

Essay, Rights of Man, 1791

Day 96

STEPHEN DECATUR, JR.

"Our country! In her intercourse with foreign nations may she always be right. But our country, right or wrong!"

Toast at a dinner in his honor, April, 1816

DAY 97

GEORGE WASHINGTON

"Guard against the postures of pretended patriotism."
Farewell Address, September 17, 1796

Today President Washington might write:

Don't let pretentious and phony so-called patriots fool you.

CHAPTER 9

A MORAL PEOPLE

No society—certainly not a free one—can survive without accepted social mores. And no social mores can reasonably be expected to survive in a culture lacking a firm moral foundation; one that's based on a proven core of tradition, wisdom and religion.

These assumptions formed the philosophical "ground zero" for our founding fathers and their generation. They simply could not—and would not care to—imagine an American society in which the lessons of millennia of man's interactions with men and God would be intentionally ignored, forgotten or, worse, rejected. They knew of no surer means to guarantee a nation that could truly flourish, prosper and be free apart from a universal recognition, celebration and practice of exalted moral standards.

While over time, a given culture's notions of morality will change, occasionally resulting in social improvement of that culture (though more often contributing to its decline). These founders, products of a civilization steeped in purposeful religion, family expectations, societal manners and super-legal constraints, understood both the benefits of a high moral bar and the dangers of moral collapse.

Read of their unquestioned loyalty to this essential basis for authentic human liberty.

DAY 98

JOHN ADAMS

"We have no government armed with power capable of contending with human passions unbridled by morality and religion. Avarice, ambition, revenge, or gallantry, would break the strongest cords of our Constitution as a whale goes through a net. Our Constitution was made only for a moral and religious people. It is wholly inadequate to the government of any other."

To the Officers of the First Brigade of the Third Division of the Militia of Massachusetts, October 11, 1798

Today President Adams might write:

Our government is not equipped to combat human passions that disregard moral decency and faith. Greed, ambition, vengeance and audacity would slice through the thickest fibers of our constitution as cleanly as a whale slices through a fish net. Our constitution was designed to lead a nation whose people are morally strong and religious; it's completely powerless to govern anyone else.

DAY 99

ALEXIS DE TOQUEVILLE

"Laws are always unstable unless they are founded on the manners of a nation; and manners are the only durable and resisting power in a people."

Democracy in America, vol 1, Chapter XVI, 1835

Today Mr. de Toqueville might write:

Laws will always prove unpredictable if they aren't built on the civility of the people because civility is the only stable strength a nation can rely on.

DAY 1 00

NOAH WEBSTER

"The virtues of men are of more consequence to society than their abilities; and for this reason, the heart should be cultivated with more assiduity than the head."

Essay, On the Education of Youth in America, 1788

Today Mr. Webster might write:

Peoples' moral character benefits society more than their talents. For this reason, more attention should be paid to developing their hearts than their minds.

DAY 1 0 1

JAMES WILSON

"It is the duty of parents to maintain their children decently, and according to their circumstances; to protect them according to the dictates of prudence; and to educate them according to the suggestions of a judicious and zealous regard for their usefulness, their respectability and happiness."

Lectures on Law: Part 3, Chapter 7: Of the Natural Rights of Individuals, 1790

Today Justice Wilson might write:

It's the parents' job to nurture their children well and, depending on their circumstances, to carefully guard and guide them based on a sensible and loving concern that they grow up to be hard-working, reputable and contented.

DAY 102

ALEXIS DE TOQUEVILLE

"[Men] grow used to everything except to living in a society which has not their own manners."

Democracy in America, vol 2, Chapter XIV, 1840

Today Mr. de Toqueville might write:

People can eventually get used to anything except living in a society where people don't share their idea of civility.

DAY 103

GOUVERNEUR MORRIS

"For avoiding the extremes of despotism or anarchy... the only ground of hope must be on the morals of the people. I believe that religion is the only solid base of morals and that morals are the only possible support of free governments."

To Lord George Gordon, June 28, 1792

Today Mr. Morris might write:

Only having hope in the moral integrity of the [American] people can avoid the extremes of government oppression or social chaos. I believe that the only firm basis for such integrity—and the only foundation able to lift a free government—is religious faith.

DAY 104

BENJAMIN FRANKLIN

"I believe there is one Supreme most perfect being. ...I believe He is pleased and delights in the happiness of those He has created; and since without virtue man can have no happiness in this world, I firmly believe He delights to see me virtuous."

Essay, Articles of Belief and Acts of Religion, 1728

Today Dr. Franklin might write:

I believe in one perfect, sovereign being. ...I believe He takes pleasure and joy in the happiness of His creation. So, since no one can be happy in this life without personal integrity, I firmly believe He is happy when I behave as I should.

DAY 105

GEORGE WASHINGTON

"It is an old adage that honesty is the best policy. This applies to public as well as private life, to states as well as individuals."

To James Madison, 1785

Today General Washington might write:

Remember that old saying, "honesty is the best policy"? Well, that works both in public and private life—and it's meant for governments as well as individuals.

DAY 106

SAMUEL WILLIAMS

"It is not necessary to enumerate the many advantages, that arise from this custom of early marriages. ...Every thing useful and beneficial to man, seems to be connected with obedience to the laws of his nature, the inclinations, the duties, and the happiness of individuals, resolve themselves into customs and habits, favourable, in the highest degree, to society. In no case is this more apparent, than in the customs of nations respecting marriage."

The Natural and Civil History of Vermont, 1809

Today Reverend Williams might write:

There's no need to count all the benefits of this tradition of marrying young. ...Everything that can help and benefit mankind seems to somehow be linked with respecting human nature. Man's urges, obligations and happiness form traditions and habits that greatly benefit society. This is most obvious in the marital traditions of a nation.

DAY 107

CHARLES CARROLL OF CARROLLTON

"Without morals a republic cannot subsist any length of time; they therefore who are decrying the Christian religion, whose morality is so sublime and pure... are undermining the solid foundation of morals, the best security for the duration of free governments."

To James McHenry, November 4, 1800

Today Mr. Carroll might write:

An immoral republic can't last very long; those who attack the Christian faith—a faith built on true and inspiring principles—sabotage the best guarantee of public morals, the most reliable evidence that free governments will survive.

CHAPTER 10

A WELCOME PIETY

"We have become accustomed to writing nobly of American ideals without either the historical accuracy or the common candor of recognizing that these ideals grew largely out of a mind and conscience that believed in God and in some eternal standards." (President Howard Lowry, College of Wooster, OH, as quoted by William F. Buckley in God and Man at Yale.)

Despite what modern thinkers may say about the role of religion in the lives and legal philosophies of our national patriarchs, religion was an essential, constructive and extremely positive component of their new model of freedom.

The Judeo-Christian religion was, in fact, acknowledged by most as the origin of social liberties and governmental constraints based on universally respected religious teachings. Love, humility, patience, peace, mutual respect, hard work, empathy with the less fortunate, loyalty, sacrificial sharing—these and many other qualities were preached and promoted by ancient practitioners of the faith our forefathers inherited and embraced.

While the founders may have differed with one another in their allegiance to particular biblical doctrines, theoretical nuances or even major theological distinctions, they undoubtedly shared in common an undeniable belief in religious faith as a key element of their American vision and a necessary deterrent to civil, if not political, anarchy.

The following words suggest convincing evidence of that reality.

JOHN ADAMS

"The second [sic] day of July, 1776, will be the most memorable epoch in the history of America. I am apt to believe that it will be celebrated by succeeding generations as the great Anniversary Festival. It ought to be commemorated, as the Day of Deliverance, by solemn acts of devotion to God Almighty.

To Abigail Adams, July 3, 1776

Today Mr. Adams might write:

July 2, 1776 will be regarded as the most exceptional date in America's history. I'm inclined to believe that our descendants will celebrate America's birthday party on this date. It should be memorialized as America's "Day of Freedom," with sincere acts of devotion to Almighty God.

BENJAMIN RUSH

"[T]he only foundation for a useful education in a republic is to be laid in religion. Without this there can be no virtue, and without virtue there can be no liberty, and liberty is the object and life of all republican governments."

Essay, On the Mode of Education Proper in a Republic, 1806

Today Dr. Rush might write:

Only religious faith can form the basis of an effective education system in a democratic republic. If you don't have religion, virtue won't grow; if virtue doesn't grow you can't have freedom—and freedom is the whole point and purpose of every republican government.

Day 110

THOMAS JEFFERSON

"God, who gave us life, gave us liberty. Can the liberties of a nation be secure when we have removed a conviction that these liberties are the gift of God? God is just, but His justice cannot sleep forever."

Essay, A Summary View of the Rights of British America; Notes on the State of Virginia, 1774

Today Mr. Jefferson might write:

The same God that gave us life also gave us freedom. But, how can a nation's freedom remain safe when we've taken away the certainty that our freedom is a gift to us from God? God's justice is certainly fair but don't expect His justice to stay asleep for long.

Day 111

GEORGE WASHINGTON

"While we are zealously performing the duties of good citizens and soldiers we certainly ought not to be inattentive to the higher duties of religion. To the distinguished character of 'Patriot,' it should be our highest glory to add the more distinguished character of 'Christian.'"

General Orders to troops at Valley Forge, May 2, 1778

Today General Washington might write:

While we enthusiastically fulfill our duties as good citizens and soldiers we should never ignore the more vital responsibilities as men of faith. To the respected title of "patriot," the noblest honor we can add is the still greater title of "Christian."

DAY 112

BENJAMIN FRANKLIN

"If men are so wicked with religion as we now see them, what would they be if without it."

To an unknown correspondent, December 13, 1757

Today Dr. Franklin might write:

If humanity is so obviously corrupt with the benefit of religion, what would they be like without it?

DAY 113

EDMUND BURKE

"I take toleration to be a part of religion. I do not know which I would sacrifice; I would keep them both: it is not necessary that I should sacrifice either."

Speech on the Bill for the Relief of Protestant Dissenters, March 7, 1773

Today Mr. Burke might say:

I take it for granted that to be religious is to be tolerant. If I had to forfeit one or the either I could not choose, so I would keep both of them since I don't have to give up either one.

DAY 114

JOHN ADAMS

"Without religion this world would be something not fit to be mentioned in polite company, I mean—Hell."

To Thomas Jefferson, April 19, 1817

Today Mr. Adams might write:

A world with no religion would become a word I could not say in polite company. That word is "Hell."

DAY 115

OLIVER ELLSWORTH

"Liberty is a word which, according as it is used, comprehends the most good and the most evil of any in the world. Justly understood it is sacred next to those which we appropriate in divine adoration."

Essay, A Landholder, No. III, November 19, 1787

Today Mr. Ellsworth might write:

The word, " freedom," in its most complete meaning, speaks to the extremes both of good and evil that exist in this world. To understand this word correctly, it's right to regard it as second only to the words used in the worship of God.

DAY 116

JOHN WITHERSPOON

"Whoever is an avowed enemy of God, I scruple not to call him an enemy of his country."

Essay, The Dominion of Providence Over the Passions of Men, May 17, 1776

Today Rev. Witherspoon might write:

I don't hesitate for a moment to call anyone who declares war on God an enemy of [America].

GEORGE WASHINGTON

"I consider it as an indispensable duty to close this last act of my official life by commending the interest of our dearest country to the protection of Almighty God, and those who have the superintendence of them to his holy keeping."

Speech at his Resignation as Commander-in-Chief of the Continental Army, Annapolis, December 23, 1778

Today General Washington might say:

I believe it is a necessary obligation to end my career as a public servant by entrusting the welfare of our precious nation to the shelter of Almighty God, and its leaders to his sacred care.

BENJAMIN FRANKLIN

"I would only request him to consider these things seriously, to wit; That wise men have in all ages thought government necessary for the good of mankind; and, that wise governments have always thought religion necessary for the well ordering and well-being of society, and accordingly have been ever careful to encourage and protect the ministers of it, paying them the highest publick honours, that their doctrines might thereby meet with the greater respect among the common people."

Letter to the "Author" of The Pennsylvania Gazette, titled "On That Odd Letter of the Drum," 1730 (as "Philoclerus")

Today Dr. Franklin might write:

All I ask is that [an anonymous letter writer] thinks seriously about the fact that (1) wise men throughout history believed that government benefits men, (2) that wise governments have always welcomed religion as a source of order and social good and, thus, (3) have always taken pains to praise and protect it's clergy and to honor them publicly above others in order that their neighbors would greatly respect the beliefs they teach.

DAY 119

ALEXANDER HAMILTON

"Moral obligation, according to [Thomas Hobbes], is derived from the introduction of civil society; and there is no virtue, but what is purely artificial, the mere contrivance of politicians, for the maintenance of social intercourse. But the reason he [ran] into this absurd and impious doctrine, was, that he disbelieved the existence of an intelligent superintending principle, who is the governor, and will be the final judge of the universe."

Essay, The Farmer Refuted, February 23, 1775

Today Mr. Hamilton might write:

So, in [Hobbes'] mind, the notion of moral duty came from the need to form a civil society where the only virtue is a fantasy, a phony façade made up by politicians to promote social interaction. But he came up with this ridiculous and disrespectful theory by, first, denying that in the end everything will be judged against an intelligent standard set by the One who rules over all.

DAY 120

GEORGE WASHINGTON

"The hand of Providence has been so conspicuous in all this that he must be worse than an infidel that lacks faith, and more wicked that has not gratitude to acknowledge his obligations..."

To Brigadier General Thomas Nelson, August 20, 1778

Today General Washington might write:

The hand of God has been so obvious in all this that only the ignorant would deny him his due. And whoever refuses to acknowledge his own duty to be grateful is even worse.

DAY 121

JAMES WILSON

"The skeptical philosophers claim and exercise the privilege of assuming, without proof, the very first principles of their philosophy and yet they require from others a proof of everything by reasoning. They are unreasonable in both points."

Lectures, 1790-1791

Today Justice Wilson might write:

Cynical intellectuals demand and practice the right to assume, with no evidence, the core beliefs of their philosophy yet they insist that their rivals offer rational proof for their opposing beliefs. Neither of these presumptions makes any sense.

SAMUEL ADAMS

"And as it is our duty to extend our wishes to the happiness of the great family of man, I conceive that we cannot better express ourselves than by humbly supplicating the Supreme Ruler of the world that the rod of tyrants may be broken to pieces, and the oppressed made free again; that wars may cease in all the earth, and that the confusions that are and have been among nations may be overruled by promoting and speedily bringing on that holy and happy period when the kingdom of our Lord and Saviour Jesus Christ may be everywhere established, and all people everywhere willingly bow to the sceptre of Him who is Prince of Peace."

Proclamation of a Day of Fast in Massachusetts, March 20, 1797

Today Governor Adams might proclaim:

Since we ought to wish happiness for the family of man, I think that the best expression of that is to humbly ask the Supreme Ruler of the world to shatter the weapons of bullies, restore freedom to the oppressed, end all warfare and promote understanding between nations by inspiring and quickly bringing about that season of pious joy when the kingdom of our Lord and Savior, Jesus Christ, will be firmly entrenched across the earth and all people will gladly yield to the rule of the One Prince of Peace.

DAY 123

GEORGE WASHINGTON

"The propitious smiles of Heaven can never be expected on a
nation that disregards the eternal rules of order and right,
which Heaven itself has ordained."

First Inaugural Address, 1789

Today President Washington might say:

*A nation that ignores the immortal decrees of peace and truth
that God has personally declared holy cannot expect to earn His
smile of approval.*

DAY 124

THOMAS JEFFERSON

"I reciprocate your kind prayers for the protection and blessing
of the common father and creator of man, and tender you for
yourselves and your religious association, assurances of my
high respect and esteem."

*To the Danbury Baptists, January 1, 1802 (The "Wall of Separation"
letter, closing paragraph)*

Today President Jefferson might write:

*I echo your kind prayers to the creator and father of all of
mankind for my protection and blessing, and offer my great
respect and admiration to you, your associates and your faith
community.*

DAY 125

ALEXIS DE TOQUEVILLE

"Despotism may govern without faith, but liberty cannot. How is it possible that society should escape destruction if the moral tie is not strengthened in proportion as the political tie is relaxed? And what can be done with a people who are their own masters if they are not submissive to the Deity?"

Democracy in America, vol 1, Chapter XVII, 1835

Today Mr. de Toqueville might write:

There may be tyrants who govern with no religious faith, but it's not possible for a free society to exist without it. Any society whose political bond is weakened without a corresponding rise in moral strength cannot possibly prevent its own collapse. How can you rescue an independent and self-governing people if they refuse to obey God?

DAY 126

GEORGE WASHINGTON

"May the father of all mercies scatter light, and not darkness, upon our paths, and make us in all our several vocations useful here, and in His own due time and way, everlastingly happy."

To a Hebrew congregation in Newport, Rhode Island, August 17, 1790

Today President Washington might write:

May the merciful father spread light rather than darkness in our paths and use our diverse talents to serve our world. May he bring eternal contentment according to his perfect time and plan.

DAY 127

ALEXANDER HAMILTON

"The sacred rights of mankind are not to be rummaged for among old parchments or musty records. They are written, as with a sun beam, in the whole volume of human nature, by the hand of the divinity itself; and can never be erased or obscured by mortal power."

Essay, The Farmer Refuted, February 23, 1775

Today Mr. Hamilton might write:

Don't look for the highest rights of man on an old bookshelf or in a dusty closet. Rather, it's as if the hand of God himself took a ray of sun to write them deep within the human spirit—and no earthly power can ever bury or erase them.

DAY 128

SAMUEL ADAMS

"[T]he importance of piety and religion; of industry and frugality; of prudence, economy, regularity and an even government; all ... are essential to the well-being of a family."

To Thomas Wells, 1780

Today Mr. Adams might write:

To become and remain healthy, a family must give priority to faith and a reverent respect for God, to career and investment and to wisdom, fidelity and a stable government.

DAY 129

ALEXIS DE TOQUEVILLE

"By the side of these religious men I discern others whose looks are turned to the earth more than to Heaven; they are the partisans of liberty, not only as the source of the noblest virtues, but more especially as the root of all solid advantages; and they sincerely desire to extend its sway, and to impart its blessings to mankind. It is natural that they should hasten to invoke the assistance of religion, for they must know that liberty cannot be established without morality, nor morality without faith; but they have seen religion in the ranks of their adversaries, and they inquire no further; some of them attack it openly, and the remainder are afraid to defend it."

Democracy in America, vol 1, Introduction, 1835

Today Mr. de Toqueville might write:

Alongside pious patriots I see men who look to earth rather than heaven for answers. These, too, love freedom as the foundation of human dignity and, even more so, as the basis for great success. Such men also want freedom for more and more people, indeed, all mankind. So, they naturally hope to partner with religion, since they realize that for freedom you need honorable people and for honorable people you need religious faith. But, because their hated rivals are religious, they dismiss it. And, because some actively oppose religion, the rest are intimidated and refuse to defend it.

Day 130

BENJAMIN FRANKLIN

"The faith you mention has doubtless its use in the world. I do not desire to see it diminished, nor would I endeavour to lessen it in any man. But I wish it were more productive of good works, than I have generally seen it: I mean real good works, works of kindness, charity, mercy, and publick spirit; not holiday-keeping,"

To Joseph Huey, June 6, 1753

Today Dr. Franklin might write:

You brought up faith and I agree it has its place in the world. I don't want to see faith fade and I wouldn't try to talk anyone out of it. Still, I wish I could see faith in action more than I do. I'm talking about genuine displays of faith, like kindness and forgiveness and working within the community—not just celebrating religious holidays.

Day 131

GEORGE MASON

"Section 16. That Religion, or the duty which we owe to our Creator, and the manner of discharging it, can be directed only by reason and conviction, not by force or violence; and, therefore, all men are equally entitled to the free exercise of religion, according to the dictates of conscience; and that it is the mutual duty of all to practice Christian forbearance, love, and charity, towards each other."

Virginia Declaration of Rights, June 12, 1776

Today Mr. Mason might write:

Section 16: [We affirm that] Worship, or the respect we owe our Maker as well as the way we fulfill it, can only be guided by reason and faith, not by force or violence. Therefore, all people have the same right to freely practice religion as advised by their own conscience. We also affirm that each of us has a Christian duty to accept, love and respect one another.

DAY 132

GEORGE WASHINGTON

"And also that we may then unite in most humbly offering our prayers and supplications to the great Lord and Ruler of Nations, and beseech Him to... promote the knowledge and practice of true religion and virtue."

Thanksgiving Proclamation, December 3, 1789

Today President Washington might proclaim:

So, together, we bow to offer our prayers and requests to the Great Lord, the King over all nations, asking him to... inspire both the understanding and the free exercise of genuine religious faith and moral integrity.

PART III
THE GENIUS

CHAPTER 11

ON PROPERTY AND PROSPERITY

America's founders recognized the importance of motivating active commerce, entrepreneurship and personal investment in the progress of America and its economy. And, having escaped the system of nobility and familial titles prevalent in Europe, they wished no part of an economic system that rewarded birth and lethargy while punishing effort, energy and enterprise.

Property ownership—even a faint hope of realistic potential for property ownership—stirs commitment, a stake in continuing and protecting prosperity. That is neither greed (although it can be) nor brazen materialism (although that's possible) nor unfair economic inequity (although there are examples). It is simply human beings responsibly looking out for themselves, their families and their neighbors while investing their intelligence, knowledge, talent, opportunities and effort to build a more prosperous and safe future for all of these.

Such commitment guarantees the growth of a strong and enthusiastic citizenry, driven to succeed and to help their neighbors and nation succeed as well. History has clearly proven that a wealthy nation governed under the will of its people and inspired by a rich tradition of charity, will become, and remain, prosperous—and will arouse other nations to do so, as well.

If we willingly ignore, reject or scorn what these men and women would teach us in our day we may willingly forfeit our own—and our children's—survival.

Read how the wisdom of these heroes can help you and me, along with our nation, to avoid that tragedy.

DAY 133

BENJAMIN FRANKLIN

"I am for doing good to the poor, but I differ in opinion of the means. I think the best way of doing good to the poor, is not making them easy in poverty, but leading or driving them out of it. In my youth I travelled much, and I observed in different countries, that the more public provisions were made for the poor, the less they provided for themselves, and of course became poorer. And, on the contrary, the less was done for them, the more they did for themselves, and became richer."

Essay, On the Price of Corn and Management of the Poor, 1766

Today Dr. Franklin might write:

I'm all for serving the poor, but I disagree on how it should be done. I think that instead of helping them become comfortable with poverty, it's best to help them escape its grasp. When I was young I traveled a lot and I noticed that the more some countries gave things to the poor the less they would do for themselves and, predictably, they became more destitute. But, when they were given less they did more for themselves and gained wealth.

DAY 134

J. HECTOR ST. JEAN DE CREVECOEUR

"If thou wilt work I have bread for thee. If thou wilt be honest, sober and industrious I have greater rewards to confer on thee—ease and independence... Go thou and work and till; thou shalt prosper provided thou be just, grateful and industrious."

What Is an American?, excerpt from "Letters from an American Farmer," 1782

Today Mr. de Crevecoeur might write:

If you will work I'll give you bread. If you will be honest, dedicated and hardworking I've got even better rewards to give you—rest and self-reliance. So, go and work your land; as long as you're fair, appreciative and productive you will succeed.

DAY 135

SAMUEL ADAMS

"The utopian schemes of leveling and a community of goods, are as visionary and impractical as those which vest all property in the crown. These ideas are arbitrary, despotic, and, in our government unconstitutional. Now, what property can the colonists be conceived to have, if their money may be granted away by others, without their consent?"

To Dennys De Berdt, January 12, 1768

Today Mr. Adams might write:

The utopian ideals of redistribution and shared wealth are as naive and impractical as those that would entrust all property to the king. These concepts are imaginary, oppressive and in [the British] government, unconstitutional. Tell me, what prosperity do you suppose Americans would have if someone else could simply take their money away and give it to others without their okay?

DAY 136

THOMAS PAINE

"Is the power who is jealous of our prosperity, a proper power to govern us?"

Essay, Common Sense, 1776

Today Mr. Paine might write:

Is it smart to be ruled by a government that resents our wealth?

DAY 137

ALEXIS DE TOQUEVILLE

"What chiefly diverts the men of democracies from lofty ambition is not the scantiness of their fortunes, but the vehemence of the exertions they daily make to improve them."

Democracy in America, vol 2, Chapter XIX, 1840

Today Mr. de Toqueville might write:

The mistaken idea that usually sidetracks men who live in democracies from reaching great heights isn't their lack of opportunity but the urgency they put into their daily efforts to increase those opportunities.

DAY 138

JAMES MADISON

"Government is instituted to protect property of every sort; as well that which lies in the various rights of individuals, as that which the term particularly expresses. This being the end of government, that alone is a just government which impartially secures to every man whatever is his own."

Essay on Property, March 29, 1792

Today Representative Madison might write:

Government is created to protect all types of property, both personal rights as well as tangible assets (what we usually mean when we say "property"). Since this is the purpose of government, the only just government is one that, without preference, diligently safeguards everything that a man rightly owns.

DAY 139

JOHN HANCOCK

"Security to the persons and properties of the governed is so obviously the design and end of civil government that to attempt a logical proof of it would be like burning tapers at noonday to assist the sun in lighting the world."

Boston Massacre Oration, March 5, 1773

Today Mr. Hancock might say:

It's so obvious that the point and purpose of civil government is to safeguard those they govern and their property that any attempt to argue the logic of it would be redundant—like lighting torches at noon to help the sun brighten the globe.

DAY 140

HORATIO BUNCE

"If you had the right to give anything, the amount was simply a matter of discretion with you, and you had as much right to give $20,000,000 as $20,000. If you have the right to give to one, you have the right to give to all; and, as the Constitution neither defines charity nor stipulates the amount, you are at liberty to give to any and everything which you may believe, or profess to believe, is a charity, and to any amount you may think proper. You will very easily perceive what a wide door this would open for fraud and corruption and favoritism, on the one hand, and for robbing the people on the other."

[c. 1831] To David Crockett, as quoted in "The Life of Colonel David Crockett" by Edward Sylvester Ellis, published 1884

Today Mr. Bunce might say:

If you [, the Congress,] had any right to dole out taxpayer money to anyone, the amount would have been entirely up to you—you could just as easily have given $20,000,000 as $20,000. And if you had authority to give to one you would have authority to give to everyone. Since the Constitution never authorizes charity, much less sets any amount, you think you're free to give any amount you want to whoever and whatever you may regard as needy. You can surely see that this practice leaves the door wide open to fraud, corruption and favoritism on one hand and stealing from taxpayers on the other.

DAY 141

THOMAS PAINE

"What we obtain too cheap, we esteem too lightly: it is dearness, only, that gives every thing its value."

Essay, The American Crisis, No. 1, 1776

Today Mr. Paine might write:

We tend to care little about what costs little. We value everything based on how steep a price we have to pay for it.

DAY 142

JAMES MADISON

"Conscience is the most sacred of all property."

Essay on Property, March 29, 1792

DAY 143

ALEXIS DE TOQUEVILLE

"In no other country in the world is the love of property keener or more alert than in the United States, and nowhere else does the majority display less inclination toward doctrines which in any way threaten the way property is owned."

Democracy in America, vol 2, Chapter XXI, 1840

Today Mr. de Toqueville might write:

Nowhere else in the world is the right to own property cherished as deeply and guarded as diligently as in the United States, and in no other nation is the majority less likely to support rules that in any way threaten the rights of property owners.

DAY 144

JAMES WILSON

"If this view [that personal liberty is provided by civil, not natural rights] be a just view of things, then the consequence, undeniable and unavoidable, is, that, under civil government, the right of individuals to their private property, to their personal liberty, to their health, to their reputation, and to their life, flow from a human establishment, and can be traced to no higher source. The connexion between man and his natural rights is intercepted by the institution of civil society. If this view be a just view of things, then, under civil society, man is not only made *for*, but made *by* the government: he is nothing but what the society frames: he can claim nothing but what the society provides."

Lectures on Law: Part 3, Chapter 7: Of the Natural Rights of Individuals

Today Justice Wilson might write:

If it were true [that civil, not natural, rights grant personal freedom] then the inevitable and undeniable result is that under a civil government a person's right to own private property and to enjoy personal freedom, health, reputation, and life are granted by men and not by a greater source. In other words, government steps between man and his natural rights. If this is true, then in a civil society a person is made both for and by the government. He is only what the society allows him to be, he can have only what society gives to him.

DAY 145

GEORGE WASHINGTON

"There is no saying to what extent an enterprising man may push his good fortune."

Speech to the New York Council of Safety, August 4, 1777

Today Mr. Washington might say:

Who knows what the limitations are of a hard-working man who makes his own luck?

DAY 146

THOMAS PAINE

Invention is continually exercised to furnish new pretenses for revenues and taxation. It watches prosperity as its prey and permits none to escape without tribute."

Essay, Rights of Man, 1791

Today Mr. Paine might write:

They're always dreaming up clever excuses for new taxes so they can get more and more revenues. [Government] views private wealth as a predator views it's prey: None are allowed to escape without surrendering their "fair share."

JOHN ADAMS

"[A]ll are subject by nature to equal laws of morality, and in society have a right to equal laws for their government, yet no two men are perfectly equal in person, property, understanding, activity, and virtue, or ever can be made so by any power less than that which created them."

Discourse on Davila - XV, 1776

Today Mr. Adams might write:

Nature forces everyone to obey the same moral laws. In every society the people have a right to laws that treat everyone the same. But no two people are perfectly equal in status, wealth, intelligence, productivity and moral values. And no one, other than their Creator, is able to make them equal.

JAMES MADISON

"As a man is said to have a right to his property, he may be equally said to have a property in his rights. Where an excess of power prevails, property of no sort is duly respected. No man is safe in his opinions, his person, his faculties, or his possessions."

Essay in The National Gazette, March 27, 1792

Today Representative Madison might write:

Just like a man is presumed to own his property, he's also presumed to own his rights. But, whenever rulers have too much power, they don't really respect ownership of any kind. [At that point] no one's opinions, soul, worth or possessions are safe.

DAY 149

THOMAS JEFFERSON

"To take from one because it is thought that his own industry and that of his father's has acquired too much, in order to spare to others, who, or whose fathers have not exercised equal industry and skill, is to violate arbitrarily the first principle of association, the guarantee to every one of a free exercise of his industry and the fruits acquired by it."

To Joseph Milligan, 1816

Today Mr. Jefferson might write:

To redistribute a person's wealth based on a belief that either his or his parents' labor has made him "too" rich, simply to rescue others whose parents (or themselves) may not have worked as hard—or honed their skills as well—unfairly violates the most fundamental principle of private property, which guarantees to everyone the opportunity to work hard and to keep the fruits of their labor.

CHAPTER 12

A ROBUST ECONOMY

Is it any wonder that a nation in its infancy, facing an enormous war debt and the practical costs of constructing both the principles and the means of governing, fears the monster of runaway debt? Clearly, there were those who adamantly insisted that financing the fledgling government with debt would guarantee a fiscally stable beginning and ever-expanding prosperity.

Thank God they did not win that debate.

Among the giants of our battle for freedom were men that were equally determined to avoid debt as the means to wealth. As a democratic republic, with no royal treasuries or armed seizures of their enemies' coffers to rely on, this upstart nation would have to depend on the industriousness of its members, the American citizens, who—having just freed themselves from unjust taxation—would find their new tax burden not lessened, but simply shifted from the crown to the stars and stripes. This time, however, the choice would be their own.

But, how does a startup government produce and sustain a robust economy? International trade, securing the land and its people against intruders and funding the infrastructure needed to grow and transport produce, feed and bring to market their livestock, harvest and process natural resources and manufacture and export commodities all would demand an immediate and shrewd fiscal policy—and the political will to implement it.

As you read these pages you will read, also, the minds of financially prudent and insightful planners. May we learn well from their good sense.

DAY 150

GEORGE WASHINGTON

"There is no practice more dangerous than that of borrowing money."

To Samuel Washington, July 12, 1797

DAY 151

THOMAS PAINE

"As parents, we can have no joy, knowing that this government is not sufficiently lasting to ensure any thing which we may bequeath to posterity: And by a plain method of argument, as we are running the next generation into debt, we ought to do the work of it, otherwise we use them meanly and pitifully."

Essay, Common Sense, 1776

Today Mr. Paine might write:

It's discouraging to realize that a spendthrift government cannot last long enough for us, as parents, to leave any assets to our heirs. It's plain to see that, rather than leave our debt for the next generation to pay, we ought to be the ones paying it off. If we don't, we shamelessly exploit our own children.

DAY 152

THOMAS JEFFERSON

"Would it not be better to simplify the system of taxation rather than to spread it over such a variety of subjects and pass through so many new hands?"

To James Madison, 1784

Today Mr. Jefferson might write:

Wouldn't it be better just to have a simple tax system than to complicate it with so many rules and sub-sections and forms and agencies?

DAY 153

GEORGE WASHINGTON

"I saw with peculiar pleasure, at the close of the last session, the resolution entered into by you, expressive of your opinion that an adequate provision for the support of the publick credit is a matter of high importance to the national honor and prosperity—in this sentiment, I entirely concur."

First Annual Address to Congress, January 8, 1790

Today President Washington might say:

I was pleased to see that you closed the last session with a resolution expressing your joint belief that it's crucial for our national economy, as well as our international honor, to allocate funds to pay off the national debt. I wholeheartedly agree with that decision.

DAY 154

JOHN ADAMS

"Frugality is a great revenue, besides curing us of vanities, levities, and fopperies, which are real antidotes to all great, manly, and warlike virtues."

To Richard Henry Lee, draft of an essay, "Thoughts on Government: Applicable to the Present State of the American Colonies," November 15, 1775

Today Mr. Adams might write:

Penny pinching earns a substantial profit as well as providing a remedy for [government's] silliness, absurdities and self-indulgences—all of which undo every noble, brave and heroic discipline.

DAY 155

THOMAS JEFFERSON

"I, however, place economy among the first and most important republican virtues, and public debt as the greatest of the dangers to be feared."

To William Plumer, July 21, 1816

Today Mr. Jefferson might write:

But I consider economic self-restraint to be at the top of the list of republican principles—and fear public debt as its greatest danger.

DAY 156

JAMES MADISON

"[T]he most productive system of finance will always be the
least burdensome."

The Federalist, No. 39 (as "Publius"), January 18, 1788

DAY 157

JAMES MADISON

"There is not a more important and fundamental principle in
legislation, than that the ways and means ought always to face
the public engagements; that our appropriations should ever go
hand in hand with our promises."

Speech in Congress, 1790

Today Representative Madison might say:

*The most important and basic legislative principle is that tax
revenues must always align with the nation's obligations and our
budget must always align with our debts.*

DAY 158

JOHN ADAMS

"The consequences arising from the continual accumulation of
public debts in other countries ought to admonish us to be
careful to prevent their growth in our own. The national
defense must be provided for as well as the support of
government; but both should be accomplished as much as
possible by immediate taxes, and as little as possible by loans."

First Annual Address to Congress, November 22, 1797

Today President Adams might say:

The consequences faced by other nations that have piled up government debt should warn us to be especially careful to not let that happen to our own. We're obligated to defend the nation and to run the federal government; both ought to be done more with current taxes and less with future debt.

DAY 159

GEORGE WASHINGTON

"As a very important source of strength and security, cherish public credit. One method of preserving it is to use it as sparingly as possible... avoiding likewise the accumulation of debt, not only by shunning occasions of expense, but by vigorous exertions in time of peace to discharge the debts... not ungenerously throwing upon posterity the burden, which we ourselves ought to bear. The execution of these maxims belongs to your representatives, but it is necessary that public opinion should cooperate."

Farewell Address, September 17, 1796

Today President Washington might say:

Prize our credit rating as a key source of [economic] strength and security. One way to safeguard it is to use credit as seldom as possible... avoid building up debt, not just by limiting expenses but by taking rigorous action (during peace time) to pay off the balance... Don't callously toss the burden we should pay onto our children and theirs. It's up to our representatives to follow these truths, but the people need to demand it, as well.

DAY 160

THOMAS JEFFERSON

"We are endeavoring, too, to reduce the government to the practice of a rigorous economy, to avoid burdening the people and arming the magistrate with a patronage of money which might be used to corrupt and undermine the principles of our government.

To Mr. [Charles de Rochemont?] Pictet, February 5, 1803

Today President Jefferson might write:

We're also trying to keep our government on a tight budget, one that won't weigh down the people and give the administration a free flow of money that could be used to corrupt and sabotage the principles on which our government was built.

DAY 161

BENJAMIN FRANKLIN

"If you know how to spend less than you get, you have the Philosopher's stone."

Poor Richard's Almanack, 1736

Today Dr. Franklin might write:

If you're smart enough to spend less than you get, you can turn lead into silver.

DAY 162

ADAM SMITH

"It is the highest impertinence and presumption, therefore, in kings and ministers to pretend to watch over the economy of private people, and to restrain their expense.... They are themselves always, and without any exception, the greatest spendthrifts in society. Let them look well after their own expense, and they may safely trust private people with theirs."

Essay, An Inquiry into the Nature and Causes of the Wealth of Nations, 1776

Today Mr. Smith might write:

It's the most patronizing insult for [presidents and other government officials] to pretend they are protecting the peoples' money and holding down costs [when] its always they that— without exception—are the biggest spenders of all. Let them manage their budget profitably and let private citizens manage their own.

DAY 163

THOMAS JEFFERSON

"But with respect to future debt; would it not be wise and just for that nation to declare in the constitution they are forming that neither the legislature, nor the nation itself can validly contract more debt, than they may pay within their own age, or within the term of 19 years."

To James Madison, 1789

Today Vice President Jefferson might write:

Instead of piling up future debt, wouldn't it be wise and fair for [our] nation to declare, as part of the constitution [we're] now writing, that neither Congress nor the whole federal government can legally sign any contract that will incur more debt than can be repaid during their generation or, in other words, within 19 years?

DAY 164

GEORGE WASHINGTON

"I entertain a strong hope that the state of the national finances is now sufficiently matured to enable you to enter upon a systematic and effectual arrangement for the regular redemption and discharge of the public debt, according to the right which has been reserved to the government. No measure can be more desirable, whether viewed with an eye to its intrinsic importance or to the general sentiment and wish of the nation."

Fourth Annual Message to Congress, November 6, 1792

Today President Washington might say:

I'm very optimistic that we now have a strong enough national economy that we can enable [Congress] to commit to a systematic and effective plan to pay off the national debt on a preset timetable, as this government is obligated to do. There's no legislative action the people want more, both because it's vitally important and because it's their top priority.

CHAPTER 13

A GLOBAL TRUST

Ardent proponents of the young nation expected the United States to quickly gain prominence in the world; the world would expect them to provide an example of leadership and hope to other nations, many of which remained mired in age-old rivalries, impoverishment and longstanding and divisive political and tribal factions.

It would not be long before the newcomer that had brazenly taken on and defeated the world's most powerful empire would be expected to replace it. And, despite struggling with their new prominence, the founders quickly learned that global leadership is a beast not to be resisted as much as tamed.

The growing temptation to lose focus would pose serious challenges to a people finally free to flex their intellectual muscle and capitalize on an emerging prominence. Would-be friends will seek to take advantage of their youth and inexperience while enemies will focus on undermining every achievement; each weakness or misstep will be skillfully exploited and courage will constantly be tested.

Thanks to the tenacity and cautious confidence of that first generation we've all inherited a proud national identity and enduring legacy. Our founding fathers envisioned, anticipated and even assumed that legacy.

From the very beginning, then, the United States was destined to assume a role of leadership—a global trust. Inattention, self-absorption, isolationist policies and abdication of that trust—or failure, over time, to maintain it—would be disastrous not just for America but for the free world.

In these pages you will read how their vision bred, empowered and, ultimately, assured it.

DAY 165

PATRICK HENRY

"Shall we gather strength by irresolution and inaction? Shall we acquire the means of effectual resistance by lying supinely on our backs and hugging the delusive phantom of hope, until our enemies shall have bound us hand and foot?"

Remarks to the Virginia House of Burgesses, Saint John's Church, Richmond, Virginia, March 23, 1775

Today Mr. Henry might say:

Will indecision and weakness make us stronger? Will we discover our courage begging from our knees, clutching an imaginary hope, until we're led away in cuffs?

DAY 166

GEORGE WASHINGTON

"The nation which indulges towards another an habitual hatred, or an habitual fondness, is in some degree a slave. It is a slave to its animosity or to its affection, either which is sufficient to lead it astray from its duty and its interest."

Farewell Address, September 17, 1796

Today President Washington might say:

A nation that allows itself to continue harboring either hatred or preference for another nation has, at some level, enslaved itself. Whether it becomes a slave to its own loathing or its own compassion, either extreme is enough to distract it from its true obligations and priorities.

DAY 167

GEORGE WASHINGTON

"In a word, I want an American character, that the powers of Europe may be convinced we act for ourselves and not for others; this, in my judgment, is the only way to be respected abroad and happy at home."

To Patrick Henry, October 9, 1775

Today General Washington might write:

Simply put, we need a distinctly American character. That's how European nations will know that we act in our own best interests, not the interests of others. I believe that's the only way we will be respected abroad and contented at home.

DAY 168

ROBERT GOODLOE HARPER

"Millions for defense, but not one cent for tribute."

Upon the retun of John Marshall, negotiating for peace with France following the XYZ Affair, June 18, 1798

DAY 169

THOMAS JEFFERSON

"I hope also that the recent results of the English will at length awaken in our Executive that sense of public honor and spirit... and will establish the eternal truth that acquiesence under insult is not the way to escape war."

To Henry Tazewell, September 13, 1785

Today Ambassador Jefferson might write:

I hope, too, that the latest venture of the English [perhaps its defeat by the Spanish in the Seige of Pensacola in 1781] will eventually inspire in our president that sense of American honor and spirit and will prove the timeless truth that war cannot be avoided by surrendering to aggression.

DAY 170

ALEXIS DE TOQUEVILLE

"No protracted war can fail to endanger the freedom of a democratic country."

Democracy in America, vol 2, Chapter XXII, 1840

Today Mr. de Toqueville might write:

Any war that goes on and on will certainly threaten the freedom of a self-governing nation.

DAY 171

GEORGE WASHINGTON

"There is a rank due to the United States, among nations, which will be withheld, if not absolutely lost, by the reputation of weakness. If we desire to avoid insult, we must be able to repel it; if we desire to secure peace, one of the most powerful instruments of our rising prosperity, it must be known that we are at all times ready for war."

Fifth Annual Message to Congress, December 3, 1793

Today President Washington might say:

A reputation for weakness will diminish, if not destroy, the admiration the world holds for these United States. If we expect to avoid contempt, we have to stand ready to oppose weakness. If we hope to ensure peace—one of the most certain guarantees of our growing economic success—all nations must be sure of our willingness to wage a necessary war.

CHAPTER 14

AN AMERICAN EXCEPTIONALISM

There's a reason why clichés become clichés; they are consistently found to be grounded in truth.

Some of us today may have forgotten what America has represented since its inception. Others, sadly, are too young to have experienced it or were never taught it by parents or teachers or books.

The term "American exceptionalism" is no misnomer; it was earned by generations of our ancestors who, in a comparatively brief lifespan, gave to the world a unique model of determination, ingenuity, innovation, teamwork, benevolence and partnership never witnessed before.

No nation so willingly offered the less fortunate of the world a champion; no nation ever forged such unity from the ranks of other nations' rejected, dejected and desperate; no nation ever displayed the means or the guts to battle tyranny side-by-side with the weak on their behalf; and no nation had ever imagined so creatively, labored so productively, learned so passionately and shared so generously than these United States of America.

The beauty is that this is exactly what our founders envisioned. It is the precise goal they set out to meet.

The question for our day is do we still value, believe in and pursue that goal?

DAY 172

THOMAS PAINE

"America is a new character in the universe. She started with a cause just and right and struck at an object vast and valuable. Her reputation for political integrity, perseverance, fortitude and all the manly excellences, stands high in the world."

Essay, The Necessity of Taxation, April 3, 1782

Today Mr. Paine might write:

The American model has never been seen before. America was born with justice and right on her side as she battled a powerful and respected foe. [Today], her reputation for political honor, determination, courage and every measure of bravery ranks her among the world's leaders.

DAY 173

GEORGE WASHINGTON

"It will be worthy of a free, enlightened—and, at no distant period—a great nation, to give to mankind the magnanimous and too novel example of a people always guided by an exalted justice and benevolence. Who can doubt, that, in the course of time and things, the fruits of such a plan would richly repay any temporary advantages which might be lost by a steady adherence to it ?"

Farewell Address, September 17, 1796

Today President Washington might write:

It will be fitting for a free and educated (and, soon, great) nation to display for the world the unique and noble example of a people forever stirred by a high sense of justice and generosity. Can anyone doubt that the benefits to be gained by remaining firm in that plan will, in due course, more than make up for any short-lived rewards that may have to be surrendered?

MERCY OTIS WARREN

"The wisdom and justice of the American governments and the virtue of the inhabitants may, if they are not deficient in the improvements of their own advantages, render the United States of America an enviable example to all of the world of peace, liberty, justice and truth."

Essay, History of the Rise, Progress, and Termination of the American Revolution, 1805

Today Mrs. Warren might write:

The good sense and fairness of the American government, together with the goodness of its people, could—if they don't fail to maximize their advantages—make the United States of America an enviable example to the entire world of peace, freedom, fairness and truth.

JOHN QUINCY ADAMS

"America, with the same voice which spoke herself into existence as a nation, proclaimed to mankind the inextinguishable rights of human nature, and the only lawful foundations of government."

Independence Day Address, July 4, 1821

Today Secretary of State Adams might say:

America still speaks today as when she declared herself a free and independent nation—when America announced to the world that all people have natural and eternal rights and that they, alone, can legitimately determine their own government.

DAY 176

THOMAS PAINE

"The reformation was preceded by the discovery of America, as if the Almighty graciously meant to open a sanctuary to the persecuted in future years, when home should afford neither friendship nor safety."

Essay, Common Sense, 1776

Today Mr. Paine might write:

America was discovered before the Protestant Reformation was launched [throughout Europe]. Maybe this land was God's gracious plan to provide a haven for those who would soon face persecution when their homelands would allow them neither fellowship nor security.

DAY 177

JOHN JAY

"I can never become so far a citizen of the world as to view every part of it with equal regard; and perhaps nature is wiser in tying us to our native soil then they are who think they divest themselves of foibles in proportion as they wear away those bonds."

To Gouverneur Morris, 1783

Today Mr. Jay might write:

I could never become so cosmopolitan that I would regard all nations the same. Maybe it's nature's wisdom that keeps us [Americans] devoted to our homeland more than those who believe that they can free themselves from social defects in direct proportion to their desire to escape the chains of their identities.

DAY 178

ALEXIS DE TOQUEVILLE

"The greatness of America lies not in being more enlightened than any other nation, but rather in her ability to repair her faults."

Democracy in America, vol 1, Chapter XIII, 1835

Today Mr. de Toqueville might write:

America's greatness doesn't come from being more brilliant than any other nation but from her ability to diagnose and fix her own mistakes.

DAY 179

JOHN QUINCY ADAMS

"Wherever the standard of freedom and independence has been or shall be unfurled, there will be America's heart, her benedictions and her prayers. But she does not go abroad in search of monsters to destroy. She is the champion and vindicator only of her own."

Independence Day Address, July 4, 1821

Today Secretary of State Adams might say:

Wherever the symbol of freedom and independence ever has been—or will be—raised up, that's where you'll find the heart, the blessings and the prayers of Americans. America doesn't go out looking for ogres to kill; but she will always fight for and protect her own.

DAY 180

THOMAS PAINE

"The cause of America is, in great measure, the cause of all mankind."

Essay, Common Sense, 1776

DAY 181

JAMES MADISON

"The eyes of the world being thus on our country, it is put the more on its good behavior, and under the greater obligation also, to do justice to the Tree of Liberty by an exhibition of the fine fruits we gather from it…"

To James Monroe, 1824

Today Mr. Madison might write:

Since the world is watching us, we must behave better than ever. We owe it to our beloved Liberty Tree to show off the delicious fruit it produces…

DAY 182

NOAH WEBSTER

"Every child in America should be acquainted with his own country. He should read books that furnish him with ideas that will be useful to him in life and practice. As soon as he opens his lips, he should rehearse the history of his own country."

Essay, On the Education of Youth in America, 1788

Today Mr. Webster might write:

Every child living in America should be familiar with the history of the United States. He should read books that will fill him with ideas to help him live life well. When he gets up to speak he should be able to tell how the United States became what it is today.

DAY 183

JOSEPH WARREN

"May we ever be a people favored of God. May our land be a land of liberty, the seat of virtue, the asylum of the oppressed, a name and a praise for the whole earth until the last shock of time shall bury the empires of the world in one common, undistinguished ruin!"

Boston Massacre Oration, March 5, 1773

Today Mr. Warren might say:

I hope we will always be a people that please God; that our nation would be the land of freedom, the home of goodness, the shelter of the needy—prized and respected by the whole world right up until the days when sudden destruction will stack all kingdoms of the world in a single, inconsequential pile of junk!

DAY 184

THOMAS PAINE

"America ever is what she thinks herself to be."

Essay, The American Crisis, No. 9, 1780

Today Mr. Paine might write:

America will always be what her people believe she can be.

CHAPTER 15

ON GOD AND GOVERNING

Having lived with the debris of sanctioned state religions in Europe, our founders were sternly against imposing an "official" American religion upon its citizens and its structures. The thought of refusing the right to participate fully in the American experiment on the basis of differing beliefs was repugnant to most who would engineer that experiment. After all, their own political rebellion against England was the result of differing beliefs with the crown.

But their collective thinking on freedom clearly evolved from a revered religious tradition, one they would hardly have ejected in designing a free government and nation. Even the avowed rationalist Thomas Paine respected the welcome effects on the whole community of Judeo-Christian standards of decency.

The expectation of the majority was to actively promote religious ideals and morals in society and in government while making it unlawful at any level of government—federal, state, municipal—to explicitly favor one form of denominational religion over others or, conversely, to exclude some for the advancement of others.

Based on the whole of their writings, their purpose cannot be re-imagined to mean squeezing government's friendship with religion and its moral teachings out of public life. It is, admittedly, a fine line we must tread but we do not preserve the founders' vision by supposing their aim was to build an impenetrable barrier between these two compatible forces.

Maybe Jefferson's "wall of separation" is better viewed as a transparent one-way curtain, allowing the light and warmth of religion to filter through a pluralistic society to the benefit of all of the people, their leaders and their culture—while screening potentially divisive dogma, biases and practices out of political deliberations.

DAY 185

JOHN ADAMS

"Human government is more or less perfect as it approaches nearer or diverges farther from the imitation of this perfect plan of divine and moral government."

Draft of a Newspaper Communication, 1770

Today Mr. Adams might write:

The governments of men move closer to, or further from, perfection in proportion to how well or how poorly they imitate God's model of moral government.

DAY 186

GEORGE WASHINGTON

"You do well to wish to learn our arts and ways of life, and above all, the religion of Jesus Christ. These will make you a greater and happier people than you are. Congress will do every thing they can to assist you in this wise intention."

To the Lenape (Delaware) Indian delegation, in reply to their request for help in promoting the work among their tribe by Christian missionary David Zeisberger, 2 May 1779

Today General Washington might write:

I would advise you to study our [European-American] culture and way of life and, most of all, the Christian faith. If you do, you will become a still greater and more contented people than you already are. And Congress will assist in any way it can to help you achieve this worthwhile goal.

DAY 187

THOMAS PAINE

"The first act of man, when he looked around and saw himself a creature which he did not make, and a world furnished for his reception, must have been devotion, and devotion must ever continue sacred to every individual man, as it appears right to him; and governments do mischief by interfering."

Essay, Rights of Man I, 1791

Today Mr. Paine might write:

Worship must have been the first action man took as he noticed himself and the abundant world waiting for him—and realized he hadn't created either one. And worship must remain a sacred duty for each individual, however he may think is right. Any government that sticks its nose into that duty causes great harm.

DAY 188

BENJAMIN RUSH

"I lament that we waste so much time and money in punishing crimes and take so little pains to prevent them... we neglect the only means of establishing and perpetuating our republican forms of government; that is, the universal education of our youth in the principles of Christianity by means of the Bible; for this Divine Book, above all others, constitutes the soul of republicanism. By withholding the knowledge of [the Scriptures] from children, we deprive ourselves of the best means of awakening moral sensibility in their minds."

Essay, in Defense of the Bible in all schools in America, 1830

Today Dr. Rush might write:

It saddens me that we waste so much time and money to punish crimes but don't bother to prevent them. We reject the only tool we've got to establish and keep our republican government-- teaching each of our kids Christian principles from the Bible. More than any other book, God's word defines the soul of a republic. When we censor the Bible we throw away the best chance we have of teaching our kids how they can awaken their consciences.

DAY 189

GEORGE WASHINGTON

"Of all the dispositions and habits, which lead to political prosperity, religion and morality are indispensable supports. In vain would that man claim the tribute of patriotism, who should labor to subvert these great pillars of human happiness, these firmest props of the duties of men and citizens. The mere politician, equally with the pious man, ought to respect and to cherish them. A volume could not trace all their connexions with private and public felicity."

Farewell Address, September 17, 1796

Today President Washington might say:

Of all beliefs and traditions that breed political success, religion and morality are most essential. Anyone claiming loyalty to America is sure to fail if he works to topple these pillars of man's contentment, these cornerstones of the citizens' duty. Like people of faith, politicians should admire and prize them. Shelves of books couldn't explain every way they influence private and public happiness.

DAY 190

NOAH WEBSTER

"It is alleged by men of loose principles or defective views of the subject that religion and morality are not necessary or important qualifications for political stations. But the Scriptures teach a different doctrine. They direct that rulers should be men "who rule in the fear of God, able men, such as fear God, men of truth, hating covetousness."

Essay, Letters to a Young Gentleman Commencing His Education, 1823

Today Mr. Webster might write:

Corrupt and ignorant men claim that religious faith and morals are irrelevant to a person's qualifications for political office. But the Bible says otherwise. The scriptures state that leaders are to be capable, honorable and contented people who fear God and govern accordingly.

DAY 191

JOHN QUINCY ADAMS

"Why is it that next to the birthday of the Savior of the World, your most joyous and most venerated festival returns on this day?... Is it not that the Declaration of Independence first organized the social compact on the foundation of the Redeemer's mission upon earth? That it laid the cornerstone of human government upon the first precepts of Christianity?"

"An Oration Delivered Before the Inhabitants of the Town of Newburyport at their Request on the Sixty-First Anniversary of the Declaration of Independence," July 4, 1837

Today Representative Adams might say:

Why is it that each year only Christmas—the birthday of the Savior of the World—is revered with more parades and parties and celebrations than is this day? Isn't it because it was on this day that the Declaration of Independence created the first social contract between equals, modeled after the Redeemer's purpose in coming to earth? And wasn't that done because in doing so this government of men would rise from the most firm foundation—the core teachings of the Christian faith?

DAY 192

GEORGE MASON

"Now all acts of legislature apparently contrary to natural right and justice are, in our laws, and must be in the nature of things considered as void. The laws of nature are the laws of God; whose authority can be superseded by no power on earth. A legislature must not obstruct our obedience to him from whose punishments they cannot protect us."

Argument, Robin v. Hardaway, 1772

Today Mr. Mason might argue:

So, all bills passed by legislators that obviously contradict mens' natural rights and justice are unlawful and must be regarded as invalid. The laws of nature are the laws of God, and no one on earth can overrule them. No lawmakers can block us from obeying the Judge from Whose sentence they can't protect us.

DAY 193

BENJAMIN FRANKLIN

"I therefore beg leave to move… that henceforth prayers imploring the assistance of Heaven, and its blessings on our deliberations, be held in this Assembly every morning before we proceed to business, and that one or more of the clergy of this city be requested to officiate in that service."

Remarks to the Consitutional Congress, June 28, 1787

Today Dr. Franklin might say:

So, I'm going to propose that from now on, we start our meeting every morning with a prayer to ask Heaven to help us and to bless our discussions before we go on to our business for that day. I also suggest that we ask one, or maybe several, of Philadelphia's clergy members to lead us in that prayer.

DAY 194

OLIVER ELLSWORTH

"We are almost the only people in the world, who have a full enjoyment of this important right of human nature. In our country every man has a right to worship God in that way which is most agreeable to his conscience. If he be a good and peaceable person he is liable to no penalties or incapacities on account of his religious sentiments; or in other words, he is not subject to persecution."

Essay, A Landholder, No. VII, December 17, 1787

Today Mr. Ellsworth might write:

We are virtually the only people on earth who can fully enjoy this key human right. In our country everyone has the right to worship God in whichever way his conscience requires. A peaceful, law-abiding person won't ever have to worry about facing penalties or prison time for his religious beliefs. In other words, he's immune to persecution.

DAY 195

BENJAMIN FRANKLIN

"I've lived, Sir, a long time, and the longer I live, the more convincing proofs I see of this truth—that God governs in the affairs of men."

Remarks to the Constitutional Convention, June 28, 1787

Today Dr. Franklin might say:

Sir, I've become an old man and the older I get the more convinced I am of this truth—God orchestrates the plans of men.

DAY 196

GEORGE WASHINGTON

"No people can be bound to acknowledge and adore the invisible hand, which conducts the affairs of men more than the people of the United States. Every step, by which they have advanced to the character of an independent nation, seems to have been distinguished by some token of providential agency."

First Inaugural Address, March 4, 1801

Today President Washington might say:

There is no society more obligated to affirm and worship the unseen hand that orchestrates men's affairs more than the people of these United States. Each step taken to improve our character as an independent nation seems to have been blessed with some act of well-timed divine provision.

DAY 197

SAMUEL ADAMS

"I firmly believe that the benevolent Creator designed the republican form of government for man."

Statement, April 14, 1785

Today Senator Adams might write:

I'm absolutely certain that our republican form of government was designed by a good and giving God.

DAY 198

GEORGE WASHINGTON

"The Commander in Chief directs that divine service be performed every Sunday at 11 o'clock in those brigades to which there are chaplains; those which have none to attend the places of worship nearest to them. It is expected that officers of all ranks will by their attendence set an example to their men."

General Orders to troops at Valley Forge, May 2, 1778

Today General Washington might order:

The Commander-in-Chief orders that religious services be held each Sunday at 11:00 in all brigades that have an assigned chaplain. Brigades without a chaplain will attend the nearest places of worship. It is expected that all officers will attend services to set an example for their men.

DAY 199

SIR WILLIAM BLACKSTONE

"Upon these two foundations, the law of nature and the law of revelation, depend all human laws; that is to say, no human laws should be suffered to contradict these... for, with regard to such points as are not indifferent, human laws are only declaratory of, and act in subordination to, the former."

Commentaries on the Laws of England: Section the Second - Of the Nature of Laws in General, 1765-69

Today Justice Blackstone might write:

All human laws depend on two fundamental laws—the law of nature and the law of divine revelation. In other words, men can't be allowed to make laws that contradict those... Except for those that are neither required nor excluded by these two, human laws simply reiterate—and are secondary to—these fundamental laws.

DAY 200

BENJAMIN FRANKLIN

"I firmly believe that without His concurring aid we shall
succeed in this political building no better than the builders of
Babel: We shall be divided by our partial local interests; our
projects will be confounded, and we ourselves shall become a
reproach and bye word down to future ages."

Remarks to the Constitutional Convention, June 28, 1787

Today Dr. Franklin might say:

*I'm certain that if we don't have God's approval and help we will
be no more successful in building this government than those who
built Babel. [Without it,] our partisan bickering and local politics
will divide us, our resolutions will be confusing and we will be
insulted and branded as failures by all generations that follow us.*

DAY 201

ELIAS BOUDINOT

"Let us enter on this important business under the idea that we
are Christians on whom the eyes of the world are now turned...
Let us in the first place... humbly and penitently implore the aid
of the Almighty God whom we profess to serve—let us
earnestly call and beseech him for Christ's sake to preside in
our councils."

Remarks to the First Provincial Congress of New Jersey, June, 1776

Today Mr. Boudinot might say:

*I suggest that we start debate on this important decision by
recognizing that, as Christians, the world is watching us... So, first
off, with humble regret let's ask for help from the Almighty God
we claim to serve. Let's sincerely appeal to Him and pray that, for
the sake of Christ, He will lead our discussions.*

DAY 202

THOMAS PAINE

"There is a single idea, which, if it strikes rightly upon the mind, either in a legal or a religious sense, will prevent any man or any body of men, or any government, from going wrong on the subject of religion; which is, that before any human institutions of government were known in the world, there existed, if I may so express it, a compact between God and man and that all laws must conform themselves to this prior existing compact, and not assume to make the compact conform to the laws."

Essay, Rights of Man, 1792

Today Mr. Paine might write:

There's one point which, if you think about it rationally—whether in legal or religious terms—will stop any man, group or government from getting the wrong idea about religion. That point is that before there were human governments, there was (if I can put it this way) a pact between God and man that all laws must respect. Don't assume you can force that first pact to fall in line with any government's laws.

DAY 203

GEORGE WASHINGTON

"Let it simply be asked, Where is the security for property, for reputation, for life, if the sense of religious obligation desert the oaths, which are the instruments of investigation in Courts of Justice? And let us with caution indulge the supposition, that morality can be maintained without religion. Whatever may be conceded to the influence of refined education on minds of peculiar structure, reason and experience both forbid us to expect that national morality can prevail in exclusion of religious principle."

Farewell Address, September 17, 1796

Today President Washington might say:

So I simply ask, what safeguard is there for one's property, reputation and life if witnesses ignore their obligation to God to tell the truth, which is integral to an effective legal system? Let's be careful when we indulge in the naïve assumption that we can nurture moral people without religious faith. Applaud the impact of a progressive education system if you will, but reason and experience both disprove the fantasy that, somehow, the morals of our nation can triumph without religious principles.

DAY 204

BENJAMIN FRANKLIN

"Do we imagine we no longer need His assistance?... if a sparrow cannot fall to the ground without His notice, is it probable that an empire can rise without His aid? We have been assured, Sir, in the Sacred Writings, that 'except the Lord build the house, they labor in vain that build it.'"

Remarks to the Constitutional Convention, June 28, 1787

Today Dr. Franklin might say:

Do we really think we no longer need His help? ...If a sparrow can't fall from the sky without Him seeing it, is it likely that a world power could emerge without His support? Sir, the Holy Scriptures promise us that "if the Lord doesn't build the house, the builders' work is pointless."

PART IV
THE DANGERS

CHAPTER 16

A FRAGILE FREEDOM

Prior to the twentieth century, virtue was esteemed in virtually all civilized societies throughout the world. This fact is reflected in most relics we've found—whether writings, art, fashions, currency, etc. Virtue as a desirable and productive contributor to social life and character was a given. Only the outliers of society—the criminal, the mischievous, the shirkers and the brazen violators of social mores—saw virtue as a negative, a hindrance to freedom, a symbol of arrogant self-righteousness.

Today, that view is so often tolerated that virtue has lost its place as a valued, respected and essential trait of a free people. Not so with the founders. To them, virtue represented nobility, or what we might today call "class."

These men and women lived in a world trapped between pompous, condescending fools and crude, vulgar adventurers. These were, for the most part, educated men for whom common sense was central to their thinking. They had to be poised and judicious to win the battles they faced. They had learned all too well the fragility of freedom; a freedom under constant threat from within and without. A freedom which, unless safeguarded by all who enjoyed it, would soon meet a slow and agonizing fate. They simply could not allow that to occur.

Common sense and a keen awareness of prior social experiments that had worked (few) as well as those that had failed (most), formed their governing priorities. Tyranny had to be made a virtual impossibility in America. Success based on anything other than hard work and social cooperation had to be regarded as offensive by all. And only a virtuous people could make and keep the freedom they yearned for and were determined to produce.

The potential price of failure was just too high. Read their warnings to the generations who would follow—including ours.

DAY 205

THOMAS PAINE

"Arms discourage and keep the invader and plunderer in awe, and preserve order in the world as well as property... Horrid mischief would ensue were the law-abiding deprived of the use of them."

Thoughts On Defensive War, 1775

Today Mr. Paine might write:

Weapons dishearten and intimidate those who terrorize and capture; weapons keep people and their property safe and the world from becoming chaotic... Horrible suffering would result if law-abiding people were forbidden to use them.

DAY 206

SAMUEL ADAMS

"Our enemies would fain have us lie down on the bed of sloth and security, and persuade ourselves that there is no danger: They are daily administering the opiate with multiplied arts and delusions; and I am sorry to observe, that the gilded pill is so alluring to some who call themselves the friends of liberty. But is there no danger when the very foundations of our civil constitution tremble?"

Essay published in The Boston Gazette (as "Candidus"), October 14, 1771

Today Mr. Adams might write:

Our opponents would prefer that we recline in laziness and safety, telling ourselves there's no danger. Every day they feed us artful lies as a sedative. It hurts to admit that their golden pill is swallowed whole by many self-described "freedom lovers," but can we really be safe while the core of our constitution is shifting?

DAY 207

EDMUND BURKE

"Tyrants seldom want pretexts... Those who have been once intoxicated with power, and have derived any kind of emolument from it, even though but for one year, never can willingly abandon it. They may be distressed in the midst of all their power; but they will never look to any thing but power for their relief."

To a Member of the [British] National Assembly, 1791

Today Mr. Burke might write:

Bullies seldom lack reasons to justify their actions... Once they've had a taste of ultimate control—even just a small morsel—and found it delicious, they can never give it up. Their power may make them miserable but the only cure they will accept for their disease is more power.

DAY 208

THOMAS JEFFERSON

"The natural progress of things is for liberty to yield and government to gain ground. As yet our spirits are free."

To Colonel Carrington, May 27, 1788

Today Mr. Jefferson might write:

It's in the nature of a free government to grab more power as a free people allows them to. So far, our spirits are still free.

Day 209

JOHN ADAMS

"Cities may be rebuilt, and a people reduced to poverty may acquire fresh property: but a constitution of government once changed from freedom, can never be restored."

To Abigail Adams, July 7, 1775

Today Mr. Adams might write:

People can rebuild cities from rubble and those impoverished by anarchy can regain their wealth, but once a constitutional government forfeits its freedom, it is lost forever.

Day 210

SAMUEL ADAMS

"It is to little purpose, then, to go about cooly to rehearse the gradual steps that have been taken, the means that have been used, and the instruments employed, to encompass the ruin of the public liberty: We know them and we detest them. But what will this avail, if we have not courage and resolution to prevent the completion of their system?"

Essay published in The Boston Gazette (as "Candidus"), October 14, 1771

Today Mr. Adams might write:

So, it does little good to calmly list, step by step, how and by what means our freedoms have been brought this close to ruin. We all know and hate each of them. But what does that accomplish if we don't have enough courage or resolve to keep them from completing their mission?

Day 211

DANIEL WEBSTER

"God grants liberty only to those who love it and are always ready to guard and defend it."

Speech, June 3, 1834

Day 212

THOMAS JEFFERSON

"Indeed, I tremble for my country when I reflect that God is just: that his justice cannot sleep for ever: that considering numbers, nature and natural means only... it may become probable by supernatural interference!"

Notes on the State of Virginia (Query VIII), 1784

Today Mr. Jefferson might write:

I really worry about my country when I reason that God's justice can't be held back forever. Even if I were to estimate just the probabilities and potential for a natural disaster [I realize that] one could happen as a result of divine intervention!

Day 213

JOHN ADAMS

"There must be a positive passion for the public good, the public interest, honor, power and glory, established in the minds of the people or there can be no republican government, nor any real liberty."

To Mercy Otis Warren, April 16, 1776

Today Mr. Adams might write:

Unless the people are intensely dedicated to their country's interests, honor, reputation and success, freedom and a republican government are impossible.

DAY 214

SAMUEL ADAMS

"If therefore a people will not be free; if they have not virtue enough to maintain their liberty against a presumptuous invader, they deserve no pity, and are to be treated with contempt and ignominy."

Essay published in The Boston Gazette (as "Candidus"), October 14, 1771

Today Mr. Adams might write:

If there are people who don't care to be free, if they aren't honorable enough to keep their freedom when an arrogant bully tries to take it, they have no right to expect pity. People like that should be despised and disgraced.

DAY 215

FISHER AMES

"Liberty is not to be enjoyed, indeed it cannot exist, without the habits of just subordination; it consists, not so much in removing all restraint from the orderly, as in imposing it on the violent."

Essay on Equality, December 15, 1801

Today Mr. Ames might write:

Liberty cannot be enjoyed, or even survive, if people will not obey just laws. Liberty is not about removing controls from the decent people, as much as it is inflicting controls on the criminals.

DAY 216

THOMAS JEFFERSON

"Timid men prefer the calm of despotism to the boisterous sea of liberty."

To Phillip Mazzai, April 24, 1796

Today Mr. Jefferson might write:

Cowardly men would rather have peace under a bully than to swim against the turbulent waves of freedom.

DAY 217

JOHN ADAMS

"Democracy never lasts long. It soon wastes, exhausts and murders itself. There was never a democracy that did not commit suicide."

To John Taylor, 1814

DAY 218

JOHN ADAMS

"Posterity! You will never know how much it cost the present generation to preserve your freedom! I hope you will make good use of it! If you do not, I shall repent of it in heaven that I ever took half the pains to preserve it!

To Abigail Adams, 1777

Today Mr. Adams might write:

Future Americans! You can't comprehend the cost paid by [prior] generations to secure your liberty! I hope you use it wisely! If not, I will watch from heaven and regret having worked so hard and endured so much sorrow to keep it alive for you!

CHAPTER 17

ON THE ALLURE OF POWER

The moral background of virtually all proponents of the Constitutional Convention that conceived and constructed our form of government taught them that there are extreme dangers in a democratic republican nation; world history, to that point, had proven that.

The most severe danger of all is some men's natural lust for influence, authority and treasure. Although the European monarchies they had finally left behind them were typically inherited, the constant threat of rival claims to the throne, attempted coups and local and regional infighting to gain the patronage of government officials kept all members of royalty on edge. Though often arrogant and self-satisfied, monarchs throughout the world had always been—and continued to be—subject to the loss of their crown and, often, their lives.

Our founders would have no part in such a failed system of governing. Divided powers, mandated and narrow restrictions on influence and limited terms in office all were part of their sensible solution to some of the risks inherent in a monarchy—risks stemming from the inevitable allure of power.

Read of our first leaders' foresight as they warned future Americans of their duty to be watchful so these deadly threats could be avoided and their constitutional model could thrive for all succeeding generations.

DAY 219

ALEXIS DE TOQUEVILLE

"A democratic government is the only one in which those who
vote for a tax can escape the obligation to pay it."

Democracy in America, vol 1, Chapter XIII, 1835

DAY 220

THOMAS JEFFERSON

"[T]he States can best govern our home concerns and the
general government our foreign ones. I wish, therefore... never
to see all offices transferred to Washington, where, further
withdrawn from the eyes of the people, they may more secretly
be bought and sold at market."

To Judge William Johnson, 1823

Today Mr. Jefferson might write:

*The states are better at managing domestic affairs and the
federal government at managing foreign ones. That's why I hope I
will never see everything controlled in Washington where, further
away from the watchful eyes of their constituents, politicos can
secretly sell themselves to the highest bidder.*

GEORGE WASHINGTON

"The spirit of encroachment tends to consolidate the powers of all the departments in one, and thus to create, whatever the form of government, a real despotism. A just estimate of that love of power, and proneness to abuse it, which predominates in the human heart is sufficient to satisfy us of the truth of this position."

Farewell Address, Septemeber 17, 1796

Today President Washington might say:

The drive to intrude [upon another's authority] wants to combine all authority in all branches into a single branch. In any form of government, this impulse will create a repressive regime. A rational perspective on the love of power, and the urge to exploit it that rules in the human heart, is enough to convince us that this concern is real.

ABIGAIL ADAMS

"I am more and more convinced that... power, whether vested in many or a few, is ever grasping, and like the grave cries, 'Give, Give.'

To John Adams, November 27, 1775

Today Mrs. Adams might write:

I'm growing more convinced that... power—whether given to a few men or to many—is never satisfied. Like the grim reaper, it screams, "Give me more! I want more!"

Day 223

JAMES MADISON

"The appointment to offices is, of all the functions and, perhaps, every other form of government, the most difficult to guard against abuse... Give it to the Executive wholly and it may be made an engine of improper influence and abuse."

Essay, Observations on Jefferson's Draft Constitution, October 15, 1788

Today Mr. Madison might write:

Of all of the tasks of a republican government—or, for that matter, of any form of government—the power to appoint officials is the hardest to protect against abuse... If the president, alone, is given that power it could become an instrument for wholesale abuse and corruption.

Day 224

ALEXANDER HAMILTON

"A fondness for power is implanted in most men and it is natural to abuse it when acquired."

Essay, The Farmer Refuted, February 23, 1775

Today Mr. Hamilton might write:

Most men have an instinctive taste for power. So, of course, they abuse it when they get it.

DAY 225

GEORGE MASON

"[C]onsidering the natural lust for power so inherent in man, I fear the thirst of power will prevail to oppress the people."

Remarks to the Virginia Ratifying Convention, June 12, 1788

Today Mr. Mason might say:

When I think about man's innate lust for power, I'm afraid that his insatiable ambition will succeed in enslaving the people.

DAY 226

SAMUEL ADAMS

"Let us disappoint the men who are raising themselves on the ruin of this country. Let us convince every invader of our freedom, that we will be as free as the constitution our fathers recognized, will justify."

Essay, The Rights of the Colonists, 1772

Today Mr. Adams might write:

Together, let's frustrate those who are advancing their political fortunes on the wreckage of our nation. Let's persuade all intruders we mean to be free, as free as the constitution our ancestors loved would demand.

BENJAMIN CHURCH

"Breach of trust in a governor, or attempting to enlarge a limited power, effectually absolves subjects from every bond of covenant and peace; the crimes acted by a king against the people are the highest treason against the highest law among men."

Boston Massacre Oration, March 5, 1773

Today Dr. Church might say:

When an executive abuses the trust of his people or tries to expand a limited power, his subjects are effectively released from any obligation or social contract [with his administration]. Crimes committed by a ruler against his people are the most treasonous violation of the highest natural law.

NATHANIEL CHIPMAN

"The legislature may proceed to the declaration of tyrannical laws; the judiciary to the pronouncing of unjust decisions; the executive furnishes the immediate instruments of tyranny and injustice."

Sketches of the Principles of Government 120-127, 1793

Today Judge Chipman might write:

The legislative branch might pass oppressive laws and the judicial branch might make unjust rulings. But only the executive branch has the authority to enforce its oppression and injustice.

DAY 229

MERCY OTIS WARREN

"It is necessary for every American, with becoming energy to
endeavor to stop the dissemination of principles evidently
destructive of the cause for which they have bled. It must be
the combined virtue of the rulers and of the people to do this,
and to rescue and save their civil and religious rights from the
outstretched arm of tyranny, which may appear under any
mode or form of government."

*Essay, History of the Rise, Progress, and Termination of the American
Revolution, 1805*

Today Mrs. Warren might write:

*Every American must use as much energy as it will take to try to
stop the spread of ideologies that will kill the dreams for which
they've sacrificed. It will take teamwork between the people and
their leaders to rescue their political and religious rights from the
kind of aggressive intimidation that will emerge regardless of
their system of government.*

DAY 230

GEORGE MASON

"Section 7. That all power of suspending laws, or the execution
of laws, by any authority, without consent of the
Representatives of the people, is injurious to their rights, and
ought not to be exercised."

Virginia Declaration of Rights, June 12, 1776

Today Mr. Mason might affirm that:

Section 7: That the authority to suspend or refuse to execute laws without the agreement of the people's representatives, no matter who issues the order, damages the rights of the people and cannot be allowed.

DAY 231

GEORGE WASHINGTON

"If, in the opinion of the people, the distribution or modification of the constitutional powers be in any particular wrong, let it be corrected by an amendment in the way which the constitution designates. But let there be no change by usurpation; for, though this, in one instance, may be the instrument of good, it is the customary weapon by which free governments are destroyed. "

Farewell Address, September 17, 1796

Today President Washington might say:

If the voters think the balance or limitations of constitutional powers are wrong in any way, those can be changed with an amendment as the constitution allows. But they must not be changed by executive order since, while it might work in one situation, it is the classic trick used to destroy governments.

Day 232

"Experience hath shewn, that even under the best forms (of government) those entrusted with power have, in time, and by slow operations, perverted it into tyranny."

Preamble to a Bill for the More General Diffusion of Knowledge, Fall, 1778

Today Mr. Jefferson might write:

Experience shows that even under the best forms of government, those that are given power have eventually—and ever so gradually—twisted it into oppression.

CHAPTER 18

A Mandated Restraint

Man's natural inclination has always been to resent and attempt to throw off any chains put on him. Whether by God, by man, by society, or even by his own conscience, people, in varying degrees, will seek what they perceive to be their own good—even at high cost to themselves or others.

The originators of these United States understood that inclination and sought tirelessly to ensure a new form of government that would minimize the impact of it. Their intuitive and novel solution was a triangular government in which all powers were specified and split into three equal but separate branches.

Collectively, the states constituted a fourth "branch," in that they were also given a share in power, which the federal government could not legally usurp or encroach upon. Though smaller and distributed, their share is, in fact, greater since they were assigned—by the Constitution—all powers not specifically granted to the federal branches.

This solution, though not entirely unique in its conception, has proven its brilliance time and again. Many brazen and arrogant attempts have been made since then to violate those set boundaries, but few have been permanently successful.

We see boundary line challenges attempted somewhat frequently in our time; our founding forefathers would advise us to keep a distrustful eye on such attempts and, if necessary, reject them at the ballot box.

DAY 233

THOMAS JEFFERSON

"It is the duty of the general government to guard its subordinate members from the encroachments of each other, even when they are made through error or inadvertence, and to cover its citizens from the exercise of powers not authorized by law."

Official Opinion, 1790

Today Secretary of State Jefferson might reason that:

In our system of government, it's mandatory to keep its component parts from intruding on each others' powers (even if the intrusion is a mistake or oversight) and to protect its citizens from any use of power the Constitution doesn't authorize.

DAY 234

JAMES MADISON

"In framing a government which is to be administered by men over men, the great difficulty lies in this: you must first enable the government to control the governed; and in the next place, oblige it to control itself."

The Federalist, No. 51 (as "Publius"), February 6, 1788

Today Mr. Madison might write:

To design a government that will be run by men who will rule over other men, you first have to give that government authority to restrain those they rule. Next, you must force it to restrain itself.

DAY 235

JOHN MARSHALL

"An unlimited power to tax involves, necessarily, a power to destroy because there is a limit beyond which no institution and no property can bear taxation."

McCullough v. Maryland, 1819

Today Chief Justice Marshall might rule that:

Limitless authority to levy taxes amounts to giving [government] the power to destroy since at some point no entity or person could pay the taxes it owes.

DAY 236

THOMAS JEFFERSON

"A wise and frugal government, which shall restrain men from injuring one another, which shall leave them otherwise free to regulate their own pursuits of industry and improvement, and shall not take from the mouth of labor the bread it has earned. This is the sum of good government, and this is necessary to close the circle of our felicities."

First Inaugural Address, March 4, 1801

Today President Jefferson might say:

A wise government—one that spends the people's money carefully—protects its citizens from hurting each other. That protection allows people to safely police their own interests and enrichment. Such a government would never take a worker's hard-earned groceries right from his family table. This is what good government is—and it's how our happiness is finally achieved.

Day 237

SAMUEL ADAMS

"The Constitution shall never be construed... to prevent the people of the United States who are peaceable citizens from keeping their own arms."

Debates and Proceedings in the Convention of the Commonwealth of Massachusetts, 1786-87

Today Mr. Adams might say:

The Constitution must never be interpreted to mean that law-abiding citizens of the United States should be prevented from owning their own firearms.

Day 238

JAMES MADISON

"The aim of every political constitution is, or ought to be, first to obtain for rulers men who possess most wisdom to discern, and most virtue to pursue, the common good of the society; and in the next place, to take the most effectual precautions for keeping them virtuous whilst they continue to hold their public trust."

The Federalist, No. 57 (as "Publius"), February 19, 1788

Today Mr. Madison might write:

The main goal of every civil constitution is, or should be, to find highly insightful leaders of the highest integrity to determine what's best for the whole country. The second goal is to exercise the most extreme caution to keep them honest for as long as they hold office.

THOMAS JEFFERSON

"They are not to do anything they please to provide for the general welfare, but only to lay taxes for that purpose. To consider the latter phrase not as describing the purpose of the first, but as giving a distinct and independent power to do any act they please which may be good for the Union, would render all the preceding and subsequent enumerations of power completely useless."

Essay, Opinion on the National Bank, 1791

Today Secretary of State Jefferson might write:

[Congress] can "provide for the general welfare" only through taxation—they cannot do whatever they feel like doing. This means they have no authority, apart from levying and collecting taxes, to take action they might think best for America. To give them that option would make the list of powers and constraints we had already specified utterly worthless.

CHAPTER 19

ON ENTITLEMENT

A nation founded on a boundless work ethic, and an economy that had multiplied many times over via a continuous flow of great ideas, technological innovation and precision development naturally looks with scorn at attempts by individuals, business or politicos to exploit that proven model.

Bur that paradigm has never told the entire story. No nation on earth has given more assistance to its own citizens, communities and struggling entrepreneurs, as has the United States. No nation has moved more fully, more abundantly, more rapidly or with more heartfelt national empathy to alleviate the sudden disasters forced upon both allies and enemies across the globe, as has the United States.

Americans can be proud of our traditional desire and determination to help those in need to get back on their feet and move forward to again be productive and proud contributors to their families and communities. It is not today, and never has been, a lack of generosity or compassion that has plagued the American conscience, though some routinely believe or allege so. Rather, it's a question of process and objective; of means and benefactor that perpetually kindles such debates.

Such controversies were not foreign to our founding generation. Madison, Jefferson, Franklin and others provided clear and rational comments on this matter. Their collective track record implies that we are foolish to ignore what they had to teach us.

DAY 240

BENJAMIN FRANKLIN

"The day you passed that act you took away from before their eyes the greatest of all inducements to industry, frugality, and sobriety, by giving them a dependence on somewhat else than a careful accumulation during youth and health for support in age or sickness. In short, you offered a premium for the encouragement of idleness, and you should not now wonder that it has had its effect in the increase of poverty?"

Essay, On the Price of Corn and Management of the Poor, 1766

Today Dr. Franklin might write:

The day you passed that law you took from them—right before their very eyes—the best of all incentives to work, save and stay focused. Instead of diligently building wealth while they were young and healthy so they could support themselves when they got old or sick, you made them dependent on another source for income. In short, by paying them you inspired them to be lazy. And you wonder why poverty has skyrocketed?

DAY 241

ALEXIS DE TOQUEVILLE

"However energetically society in general may strive to make all the citizens equal and alike, the personal pride of each individual will always make him try to escape from the common level, and he will form some inequality somewhere to his own profit."

Democracy in America, vol 2, Chapter XVI, 1840

Today Mr. de Toqueville might write:

No matter how zealously the social mainstream works to make everyone equal and identical, each man's ego will inevitably drive him to try to get ahead of his competition.

DAY 242

DAVID CROCKETT

"We have the right as individuals to give away as much of our own money as we please in charity; but as members of Congress we have no right to appropriate a dollar of the public money."

Speech in the US House of Representatives, [c. 1831], as paraphrased in "The Life of Colonel David Crockett" by Edward Sylvester Ellis, published 1884

Today Congressman Crockett might say:

We have the right, as private individuals, to donate to charity as much of our own money as we want. But as members of Congress we have no right to give away a single dollar of the taxpayers' money.

Day 243

THOMAS JEFFERSON

"I think we have more machinery of government than is necessary, too many parasites living on the labor of the industrious."

To William Ludlow, 1824

Today Mr. Jefferson might write:

In my opinion, we've got far more government bureaucracies than we need and too many freeloaders living off of the sweat of the hardworking.

Day 244

JAMES MADISON

"Charity is no part of the legislative duty of the government."

Speech to the House of Representatives, 1794

Today Representative Madison might say:

What does government's obligation to make laws have to do with charity? Nothing.

DAY 245

BENJAMIN FRANKLIN

"To relieve the misfortunes of our fellow creatures is concurring with the Deity, 'tis Godlike, but if we provide encouragements for laziness, and supports for folly, may it not be found fighting against the order of God and Nature, which perhaps has appointed want and misery as the proper punishments for and cautions against as well as necessary consequences of idleness and extravagancy."

To Peter Collinson, May 9, 1753

Today Dr. Franklin might write:

It's godly and pleasing to Him to ease the suffering of our fellow man. But if we willingly encourage laziness and enrich stupidity, aren't we guilty of opposing both God and Nature? Maybe it has always been their [joint] plan that poverty and misery would be the suitable consequence of, and warning against, laziness and overindulgence.

DAY 246

GEORGE WASHINGTON

"Nothing is a greater stranger to my breast, or a sin that my soul more abhors, than that black and detestable one, ingratitude."

To Governor Dinwiddie, May 29, 1754

Today Major Washington might write:

I can't think of anything my soul finds more repulsive, more wicked or more to be hated than an ungrateful heart.

DAY 247

JAMES MADISON

"A just security to property is not afforded by that government under which unequal taxes oppress one species of property and reward another species."

Essay on Property, March 29, 1792

Today Representative Madison might write:

Any government that levies taxes unevenly to penalize one class of property while rewarding another does not provide fair safeguards for either.

DAY 248

BENJAMIN FRANKLIN

"Under all these obligations are our poor modest, humble, and thankful; and do they use their best endeavours to maintain themselves, and lighten our shoulders of this burden?—On the contrary, I affirm that there is no country in the world in which the poor are more idle, dissolute, drunken, and insolent."

Essay, On the Price of Corn and Management of the Poor, 1766

Today Dr. Franklin might write:

With all of these government entitlements [in British America], are the "takers" among us humble and grateful? And do they try their best to earn their own living and ease the burden of those who work and pay taxes? Hardly! I can confirm that there is no other nation [than England] in which the idle are more shiftless, belligerent, reckless and rude.

Day 249

ALEXIS DE TOQUEVILLE

"As for me, I am deeply a democrat; this is why I am in no way a socialist. Democracy and socialism cannot go together. You can't have it both ways."

Notes for a Speech on Socialism, 1848

Today Mr. de Toqueville might write:

Since I am a firm believer in democracy there's no way I could be a socialist. Democracy and socialism can't co-exist. You can't have it both ways.

Day 250

JAMES MADISON

"I cannot undertake to lay my finger on that article of the Constitution which granted a right to Congress of expending, on objects of benevolence, the money of their constituents."

Speech to the House of Representatives, January 10, 1794

Today Representative Madison might say:

I can't quite put my finger on the precise article in the Constitution that gives Congress the right to spend their constituents' taxes on charity.

DAY 251

THOMAS PAINE

"There is a kind of bastard generosity which, by being extended to all men, is as fatal to society, on one hand, as the want of true generosity is on the other. A lax manner of administering justice, falsely termed moderation, has a tendency both to dispirit public virtue and promote the growth of public evils."

Essay, The American Crisis, 1777

Today Mr. Paine might write:

There's a sort of perverted notion of charity that, if given to everyone, will kill a society just as much as no charity at all. Tolerance in handing out justice (deceptively called "fairness") tends to both stifle public decency and promote public corruption.

DAY 252

BENJAMIN FRANKLIN

"Repeal that [welfare] law, and you will soon see a change in their manners. 'Saint' Monday and 'Saint' Tuesday, will soon cease to be holidays. 'Six days shalt thou labor,' though one of the old commandments long treated as out of date, will again be looked upon as a respectable precept; industry will increase, and with it plenty among the lower people; their circumstances will mend, and more will be done for their happiness by inuring them to provide for themselves, than could be done by dividing all your estates among them."

Essay, On the Price of Corn and Management of the Poor, 1766

Today Dr. Franklin might write:

Repeal that welfare law and you'll see a different attitude. Monday and Tuesday will no longer be "holy days" [like Sunday]. The ancient commandment, "You will work six days," long thought to be old-fashioned, will once again be respected as a sound practice. Production will increase and the poor will earn more and be able to ease their financial woes. Making them provide for themselves would help them more than if you redistributed all of your riches among them.

DAY 253

GEORGE WASHINGTON

"Your love of liberty—your respect for the laws—your habits of industry—and your practice of the moral and religious obligations, are the strongest claims to national and individual happiness."

To the residents of Boston, October 27, 1789

Today President Washington might write:

If you love freedom, if you respect the law, if you work hard, if you fulfill your moral and spiritual duties, you have earned the right to enjoy both national and personal contentment.

DAY 254

ALEXIS DE TOQUEVILLE

"It is the dissimilarities and inequalities among men which give rise to the notion of honor; as such differences become less, it grows feeble; and when they disappear, it will vanish too."

Democracy in America, vol 2, Chapter XVIII, 1840

Today Mr. de Toqueville might write:

It's the differences and inequities between people that drive the very idea of honor. When these differences fade, honor weakens. When the differences disappear, so will honor.

CHAPTER 20

ON VIRTUE AND FREEDOM

Our earliest generation was virtually unanimous on the basis for individual and national freedom. Their vision required an absolute and uncompromising dedication to personal virtue. To them, "virtue" summarized genuine morality, nobility of character, integrity, work ethic, patriotism, religious faith and so much more. In their resolute opinion, freedom was inextricably and permanently dependent on it.

It was no coincidence that the fruit of their labors, the U.S. Constitution, has been recognized internationally for centuries as a paradigm of governmental virtue. Neither is it coincidental that the founders sought, to the smallest detail, to construct an American society where virtue ruled, where mutual respect, courtesy and cooperation with each other was apparent and where the relationship between the people and their leaders was peaceful, proactive and collaborative. These objectives demanded a shared virtue and the freedom to nurture it.

The remarks noted in the following pages ardently encourage and proclaim that vision and, as with other challenges all generations of free men face, give us pause to think seriously about our own roles in achieving it.

DAY 255

SAMUEL ADAMS

"He therefore is the truest friend to the liberty of his country who tries most to promote its virtue, and who, so far as his power and influence extend, will not suffer a man to be chosen into any office of power and trust who is not a wise and virtuous man... The sum of all is, if we would most truly enjoy this gift of Heaven, let us become a virtuous people."

Essay published in The Advertiser, 1748

Today Mr. Adams might write:

The closest friend to his country and its freedom, then, is the one who tirelessly promotes moral character and won't—to the extent he can prevent it—let a careless crook be voted into office and trusted with power. The bottom line is, if we really hope to continue enjoying this gift of God we, ourselves, have to be honorable.

DAY 256

FISHER AMES

"The known propensity of a democracy is to licentiousness which the ambitious call, and ignorant believe, to be liberty."

Remarks to the Massachusetts Ratifying Convention, 1788

Today Mr. Ames might say:

We know that a democracy will lean towards immorality. Attention seekers call this "true freedom"—and the ignorant buy that delusion.

DAY 257

JOHN ADAMS

"The only foundation of a free constitution is pure virtue, and if this cannot be inspired into our people in a greater measure than they have it now, they may change their rulers and the forms of government, but they will not obtain a lasting liberty. They will only exchange tyrants and tyrannies."

To Zabdiel Adams, June 21, 1776

Today Mr. Adams might write:

Undeniable integrity is the only basis for a free constitution. If our citizens can't be inspired more than they are, they can elect new leaders and choose a new form of government all they want, but they will never have a lasting freedom; they'll just trade one oppressive regime for another.

DAY 258

EDMUND BURKE

"What is liberty without…virtue? It is…madness, without restraint."

To a Member of the National Assembly, 1791

Today Mr. Burke might write:

What is freedom without moral integrity? It's like a lunatic unleashed.

DAY 259

DANIEL WEBSTER

"To preserve the government we must also preserve morals.
Morality rests on religion; if you destroy the foundation, the
superstructure must fall. When the public mind becomes
vitiated and corrupt, laws are a nullity and constitutions are
waste paper."

Speech, July 4, 1802

Today Mr. Webster might say:

*We can't save government unless we also save morality. The
bedrock of morality is faith; if you destroy the bedrock, the
building will collapse. When the minds and hearts of the people
grow perverted and corrupt, laws become useless and
constitutions become like toilet paper.*

DAY 260

GEORGE WASHINGTON

"Arbitrary power is most easily established on the ruins of
liberty abused to licentiousness."

Circular to the States, June 8, 1783

Today Mr. Washington might write:

*The easiest route to absolute tyranny is to build it on the ruins of a
free people absorbed in shameless self-gratification.*

DAY 261

SAMUEL ADAMS

"I thank God that I have lived to see my country independent and free. She may long enjoy her independence and freedom if she will. It depends on her virtue."

To Richard Henry Lee, March 28, 1783

DAY 262

NOAH WEBSTER

"It is an object of vast magnitude that systems of education should be adopted and pursued which may not only diffuse a knowledge of the sciences but may implant in the minds of the American youth the principles of virtue and of liberty and inspire them with just and liberal ideas of government and with an inviolable attachment to their own country."

Essay, On the Education of Youth in America, 1788

Today Mr. Webster might write:

It's extremely important to embrace and practice educational standards that will not merely spread scientific knowledge but can also plant firmly in young American minds the value of character and freedom and inspire them with both fair and innovative theories of government as well as an unwavering loyalty to their country.

DAY 263

RICHARD HENRY LEE

"It is certainly true that a popular government cannot flourish
without virtue in the people."

To Colonel Martin Pickett, 1786

DAY 264

BENJAMIN FRANKLIN

"Only a virtuous people are capable of freedom. As nations
become corrupt and vicious, they have more need of masters."

To the Abbés Chalut and Arnaud, April 17, 1787

Today Dr. Franklin might write:

*Only people that are morally strong are capable of freedom.
When a nation's masses have grown dishonest and nasty what
they really need is a disciplinarian.*

DAY 265

PATRICK HENRY

"Show me that age and country where the rights and liberties
of the people were placed on the sole chance of their rulers
being good men, without a consequent loss of liberty! I say that
the loss of that dearest privilege has ever followed, with
absolute certainty, every such mad attempt."

*Remarks to the Federal Constitution, Virginia Ratifying Convention,
1788*

Today Mr. Henry might say:

Show me the time and place where the people didn't lose their freedom when they gambled away their rights and freedoms by presuming that their rulers would be morally respectable! As far as I'm concerned, losing that most precious privilege has always followed, without exception, every example of such insanity.

DAY 266

SAMUEL ADAMS

"If virtue and knowledge are diffused among the people, they will never be enslaved. This will be their great security."

To James Warren, February 12, 1779

Today Mr. Adams might wriite:

If moral integrity and awareness are commonplace among the people [of this nation] they'll never become enslaved by anyone. These qualities will keep their freedom secure.

DAY 267

JOSEPH STORY

"Republics are created by the virtue, public spirit, and intelligence of the citizens. They fall, when... the profligate are rewarded, because they flatter the people, in order to betray them."

Commentaries on the Constitution, 1833

Today Justice Story might write:

Republics are built by the morals, community spirit and intellect of their people. Republics collapse when... scoundrels are rewarded; they smooth-talk the people, then turn on them.

DAY 268

DANIEL WEBSTER

"Liberty exists in proportion to wholesome restraint."

Speech at the Charleston Bar Dinner, May 10, 1847

Today Senator Webster might say:

Freedom exists only to the extent that a healthy self-control is exercised.

DAY 269

SAMUEL ADAMS

"No people will tamely surrender their liberties, nor can any be easily subdued, when knowledge is diffused and virtue is preserved. On the contrary, when people are universally ignorant, and debauched in their manners, they will sink under their own weight without the aid of foreign invaders."

To James Warren, November 4, 1775

Today Mr. Adams might write:

When the people are informed and their honor is preserved, they won't timidly surrender their freedoms or be easily intimidated. But, when people are totally ignorant and immoral they will destroy themselves without the help of foreign intruders.

JOHN WITHERSPOON

"Nothing is more certain than that a general profligacy and corruption of manners make a people ripe for destruction. A good form of government may hold the rotten materials together for some time, but beyond a certain pitch, even the best constitution will be ineffectual, and slavery must ensue."

Essay, The Dominion of Providence Over the Passions of Men, May 17, 1776

Today Rev. Witherspoon might write:

It's absolutely true that a general carelessness and rudeness makes a people ripe for ruin. A good government might hold the rotting pieces together for a while but, at some point, even the best constitution will fail and slavery will become inevitable.

EDMUND BURKE

"Men are qualified for civil liberty in exact proportion to their disposition to put moral chains upon their own appetites."

To a Member of the [British] National Assembly, 1791

Today Mr. Burke might write:

People deserve their civil liberties to the same degree that they are willing to curb their own selfish cravings.

DAY 272

FISHER AMES

"Men are often false to their country and their honor, false to their duty and even to their interest, but multitudes of men are never long false or deaf to their passion."

Speech in Boston, February 8, 1800

Today Mr. Ames might say:

People are often unfaithful to their country, unfaithful to their responsibilities, even unfaithful to their own best interests. But there are plenty of men who aren't likely to be unfaithful—or indifferent—toward their passions.

DAY 273

GEORGE WASHINGTON

"'Tis substantially true, that virtue or morality is a necessary spring of popular government. The rule, indeed, extends with more or less force to every species of free government. Who, that is a sincere friend to it, can look with indifference upon attempts to shake the foundation of the fabric?"

Farewell Address, September 17, 1796

Today President Washington might say:

It's very true to say that virtue, or morality, is essential to create a government of the people. In fact, that rule applies, more or less, to every type of free government. What honest advocate of truth can ignore attempts to shake the framework [of our government] to its core?

DAY 274

SAMUEL WEST

"The most perfect freedom consists in obeying the dictates of right reason, and submitting to natural law. When a man goes beyond or contrary to the law of nature and reason, he becomes the slave of base passions and vile lusts... The servants of sin and corruption are subjected to the worst kind of tyranny in the universe. Hence we conclude that where licentiousness begins, liberty ends."

Election Sermon; The True Principles of Government, May 29, 1776

Today Reverend West might say:

True freedom comes from obeying the demands of sound reasoning and giving in to the laws of nature. A man who rebels against natural law or reason surrenders to his shameful urges and repulsive cravings. ...Such slaves to indecent and corrupt masters are victims of the nastiest oppression in the universe. And so, we reason that where immorality begins, freedom ends.

DAY 275

BENJAMIN FRANKLIN

"I agree to this Constitution, with all its faults—if they are such... and I believe, farther, that this is likely to be well administered for a course of years, and can only end in despotism, as other forms have done before it, when the people shall become so corrupted as to need despotic government, being incapable of any other."

Remarks to the Constitutional Convention, Septemeber 17, 1787

Today Dr. Franklin might write:

Even with its many so-called faults, I approve this Constitution. More than that, I'm convinced that it will probably be well-managed for years to come. But it can only end up being replaced by a tyrant—as so many governments before this one—when its people become so immoral, so easily duped, so "free" that they need a bully to lead them because they can't be led by anyone else.

PART V
THE CARETAKERS

CHAPTER 21

ON POLITICAL DISCOURSE

Verbal tirades, assaults and lies in the course of political dialog are nothing new. With scandalous vehemence, our founders and earliest politicians decried their opponents and their parties, supporters and allies with equal vigor. Many of their debates, formal or not, are the stuff of legend, immortalized in our congressional archives.

Nevertheless, the less strident among our founding fathers longed for principled political discourse that offered ideas not ideology. They preferred substance over style and sense over inflammatory rhetoric.

Like today, the political arguments of our founders mimicked those of the ancient Greek politicos, often divided into two tactical schools—either the pragmatic conservative or the emotional liberal. And like them, we still struggle with the same controversial and conflicting methods of dialog, often losing sight of the real issues— and their profound implications—along the way.

As much as these strong-willed and competitive men delighted in the effect of well-timed sarcasm, an exaggerated mocking gesture or confrontational interrogation, they recognized that some of their political peers were adept at employing rhetorical tricks and opted to rely on them, rather than on sensible and open dialog, to get applause—and votes. In the founders' eyes, such tactics branded these men as unfit to hold the public's trust.

Read some of this sage advice from our founding era to get a better insight into rhetorical tricks we, as voters, ought to recognize—and reject.

DAY 276

THOMAS JEFFERSON

"I suppose, indeed, that in public life a man whose political principles have any decided character and who has energy enough to give them effect must always expect to encounter political hostility from those of adverse principles..."

To Richard M. Johnson, 1808

Today President Jefferson might write:

Of course, I assume that any public official whose political morals have shown true integrity and has enough courage to live by them must always expect to face political hatred from those who reject those morals.

DAY 277

THOMAS PAINE

"There are two distinct species of popularity; the one excited by merit, the other by resentment."

Essay, Rights of Man I, 1791

Today Mr. Paine might write:

There are two types of popular support; the first comes from your own success, the other from stirring up resentment of another's.

DAY 278

EDMUND BURKE

"They defend their errors as if they were defending their inheritance."

Speech on the Independence of Parliament, 1780

DAY 279

JOHN QUINCY ADAMS

"Of the two great political parties which have divided the opinions and feelings of our country, the candid and the just will now admit that both have contributed splendid talents, spotless integrity, ardent patriotism, and disinterested sacrifices to the formation and administration of this government, and that both have required a liberal indulgence for a portion of human infirmity and error."

Inaugural Address, March 4, 1825

Today President Adams might say:

Regarding the two leading political parties that have split the opinions and emotions of our nation, fair and honest people have to admit that both [parties] have demonstrated enough impressive skills, flawless character, fervent patriotism and impartial sacrifices to form and lead this government—but that each has also needed a healthy dose [of voter patience] for their human blunders and weakness.

Day 280

THOMAS JEFFERSON

"Bigotry is the disease of ignorance, of morbid mind...
Education & free discussion are the antidotes of both."

To John Adams, August 1, 1816

Today Mr. Jefferson might write:

*Prejudice is an illness resulting from ignorance and negative
thinking... Both are cured by education and open discussion.*

Day 281

SAMUEL ADAMS

"How strangely will the tools of a tyrant pervert the plain
meaning of words!"

To John Pitts, January 21, 1776

Today Mr. Adams might write:

*It's unbelievable how convincingly a scheming bully can distort
even the most obvious meaning of simple words!*

Day 282

GEORGE WASHINGTON

"When one side of a story is heard, and often repeated, the
human mind becomes impressed with it, insensibly."

To Edmund Pendleton, January 22, 1795

Today President Washington might write:

When people hear only one side, over and over, they tend to carelessly assume it to be true.

Day 283

JOHN ADAMS

"Is it better to apply, as this writer and his friends do, to the basest passions in the human breast——to their fear, their vanity, their avarice, ambition, and every kind of corruption?"

Novanglus I, January 23, 1775 ("Novanglus," meaning New Englander, was a pen name)

Today Mr. Adams might write:

Do you think it's better to imitate those who, by their inflammatory words, bring out the very worst in people—fear and pride, greed, lust for control and every twisted practice known to man?

Day 284

THOMAS JEFFERSON

"I never saw an instance of one of two disputants convincing the other by argument."

To John Taylor, June 1, 1798

Today President Jefferson might write:

I've yet to see even one example of a rival convincing his opponent by the brilliance of his argument.

DAY 285

BENJAMIN FRANKLIN

"A spoonful of honey will catch more flies than a gallon of vinegar."

Poor Richard's Almanack, 1745

DAY 286

GEORGE WASHINGTON

"[T]here is nothing which can have a more powerful tendency than the careful cultivation of harmony, combined with a due regard to stability, in the public councils."

Fourth Annual Message to Congress, November 6, 1792

Today President Washington might say:

Patiently building a lasting rapport is the most powerful tool of government.

DAY 287

THOMAS JEFFERSON

"I know too well from experience the progress of political controversy, and the exacerbation of spirit into which it degenerates, not to fear for the continuance of your mutual esteem. One piquing thing said draws on another, then a third, and always with increasing acrimony, until all restraint is thrown off, and it becomes difficult for yourselves to keep clear of the toils in which your friends will endeavor to interlace you, and to avoid the participation in their passions which they will endeavor to produce. A candid recollection of what you know of each other will be the true corrective."

To Colonel James Monroe, February 18, 1808

Today President Jefferson might write:

I know all too well from personal experience how political disputes decay friendships and fray nerves, so I worry that your mutual respect wll suffer. One insult leads to another, then another— each one more malicious than the previous, until it becomes a free-for-all, at which point it's hard to distance yourself from it and to avoid getting sucked into the toxic rants your supporters try to provoke you into. Honestly recalling the reasons for your friendship is the only cure.

DAY 288

ALEXANDER HAMILTON

"Why has government been instituted at all? Because the passions of men will not conform to the dictates of reason and justice without constraint."

The Federalist, No. 15 (as "Publius"), December 1, 1787

Today Mr. Hamilton might write:

What purpose does government serve? It serves to restrain those whose passions refuse to comply with the impartial demands of common sense.

FISHER AMES

"We are, heart and soul, friends to the freedom of the press. It is however, the prostituted companion of liberty, and somehow or other, we know not how, its efficient auxiliary. They are in England, they are here, they are everywhere. It is a precious pest, and a necessary mischief, and there would be no liberty without it."

Review of the Pamphlet on the State of the British Constitution, 1807

Today Mr. Ames might write:

We wholeheartedly support freedom of the press. But the media is liberty's harlot and, somehow (though we don't undestand how), its helpful ally. That's true in the United States and in England and everywhere else. The media is a familiar nuisance and a necessary meddler—and there can be no real freedom without them.

Day 290

ALEXIS DE TOQUEVILLE

"In order to enjoy the inestimable benefits that the liberty of the press ensures, it is necessary to submit to the inevitable evils it creates."

Democracy in America, vol 1, Chapter XI, 1835

Today Mr. de Toqueville might write:

To continue to enjoy the countless benefits of a free press, we need also to face the fact that untold misery will sometimes be unavoidable.

DAY 291

GEORGE WASHINGTON

"In disputes be not so desirous to overcome as not to give liberty to each one to deliver his opinion."

Essay, Rules of Civility, 1745

Today Mr. Washington might write:

When arguing politics, don't be so determined to win the argument that you refuse to give others a chance to give their opinions, too.

DAY 292

THOMAS JEFFERSON

"But every difference of opinion is not a difference of principle."

First Inaugural Address, March 4, 1801

DAY 293

SARAH UPDIKE GODDARD

"[E]very one who takes delight in publicly or privately taking away any person's good name, or striving to render him ridiculous, are in the fall of bitterness, and in the bonds of iniquity, whatever their pretences may be for it."

To William Goddard [son], 1765

Today Mrs. Goddard might write:

Everyone who enjoys stealing someone's good name, who is determined to make another person the object of ridicule—whether it's done in public or in private—exposes their own bitterness; they are imprisoned by their own corruption, no matter what excuses they may make.

DAY 294

JOHN QUINCY ADAMS

"To believe all men honest would be folly. To believe none so, is something worse."

To William Eustis, June 22, 1809

Today Mr. Adams might write:

It's foolish to believe that all people are honest. But it's idiotic to believe that none are.

DAY 295

THOMAS PAINE

"The little wranglings and indecent contentions of personal party are as dishonorable to our characters as they are injurious to our repose."

Essay, The American Crisis, No, 13, 1783

Today Mr. Paine might write:

The petty bickering and rude and personal assaults are as much an insult to our honor as they are upsetting to our composure.

THOMAS JEFFERSON

"When angry, count ten before you speak; if very angry, a
hundred."

Essay, A Decalogue of Canons for Observations in Practical Life,
Feburary 21, 1825

CHAPTER 22

A VIGILANT ELECTORATE

Our lives are full enough already. "There's not enough hours in the day," is our common complaint. Still, we willingly jam into our agendas time to relax, to be entertained, to recreate. And we should; we need to. But in the process we often squeeze out those priorities that have true and ongoing value and significance.

The founders regretted that reality. They understood it, of course. Like prominent people in our day, the demands on their time and attention were, at times, overwhelming. But they also realized that ignorance does not, in fact, produce bliss. Quite the opposite; ignorance tolerates—and eventually yields to—a covert kind of self-tyranny.

There was, and is, only one remedy for ignorance in a free society. Only a watchful people will be ready to sound—and heed—the alarm when subtle signs forecast a pending disaster, a rear assault on our freedoms, on our forefathers' legacy, on our historic greatness. In other words, if our generation surrenders these treasures because of deliberate ignorance, we have no one to accuse but ourselves.

Having outlasted a grueling, lengthy and terrible—but necessary—war, the founding generation of Americans was extreme in its zeal to protect their hard-won prize—*their* democracy. If those who follow fail to appreciate and respect the need for constant vigilance in questioning the ambitions of their government and those who seek to lead them, it would hasten the eventual doom of their promising new offspring.

This was one of our founders' deepest frustrations and greatest fears. Read the anxiety in their words and be warned—and suspicious.

DAY 297

JOHN ADAMS

"Because power corrupts, society's demands for moral authority and character increase as the importance of the position increases."

Uncited quote, The Adams Memorial (adamsmemorial.org)

DAY 298

THOMAS JEFFERSON

"If a nation expects to be ignorant and free, in a state of civilization, it expects what never was and never will be. The functionaries of every government have propensities to command at will the liberty and property of their constituents. There is no safe deposit for these but with the people themselves; nor can they be safe with them without information."

To Colonel Charles Yancey, January 6, 1816

Today Mr. Jefferson might write:

People who imagine that in a civil state they can be both ignorant and free imagine the impossible. It will never happen. Every government bureaucrat is tempted to steal the freedom and property of their constituents any time they want. These can't be safe anywhere but in the hands of the people themselves—and they can't be safe with the people, either, if they fail to pay attention and learn the relevant facts.

Day 299

DANIEL WEBSTER

"I fear that they may place too implicit a confidence in their public servants, and fail properly to scrutinize their conduct; that in this way they may be made the dupes of designing men, and become the instruments of their own undoing."

Comments at a public dinner, May 23, 1837 (Writings and Speeches, Vol. 2, June 1, 1837)

Today Senator Webster might write:

I'm afraid the people just assume that their public servants are making good decisions and utterly fail to keep an eye on what they're doing. This is how they can be suckered by conniving men —and bring about their own ruin.

Day 300

JAMES MADISON

"There are more instances of the abridgment of the freedom of the people by gradual and silent encroachments of those in power than by violent and sudden usurpations."

Remarks to the Virginia Ratifying Convention, 1788

Today Mr. Madison might write:

There are more examples of people losing their freedom by the slow and undetectable expansion of government power than by sudden and bloody insurrections.

DAY 301

ALEXIS DE TOQUEVILLE

"The will of man is not shattered, but softened, bent, and guided; men are seldom forced by it to act, but they are constantly restrained from acting. Such a power does not destroy, but it prevents existence: it does not tyrannize, but it compresses, enervates, extinguishes, and stupefies a people, till each nation is reduced to nothing better than a flock of timid and industrious animals, of which the government is the shepherd."

Democracy in America, vol 2, Chapter VI, 1840

Today Mr. de Toqueville might write:

A crafty government weakens the determination of its people. Though their will may survive, it becomes pliable, unsteady, submissive, no longer willing to resist. A calculating power cannot kill men's dreams but it can deaden them, shrink them, stymie and even douse their desires. When the promise of a people is nullified, men and women are reduced to mere droids, re-designed and re-programmed for the masters' purposes.

DAY 302

PATRICK HENRY

"We are not weak if we make a proper use of those means which the God of Nature has placed in our power. ... The battle, sir, is not to the strong alone; it is to the vigilant, the active, the brave."

Remarks to the Virginia House of Burgesses, Saint John's Church, Richmond, Virginia, March 23, 1775

Today Mr. Henry might say:

With due respect, Sir, it isn't a sign of weakness to rely on the common sense the Creator has given us. ...Conflicts are won not only by the strong but by those who remain alert, involved and courageous.

DAY 303

GEORGE WASHINGTON

"Truth will ultimately prevail where there are pains taken to bring it to light."

To Charles Mynn Thurston, 1794

Today President Washington might write:

Truth will always win when people are determined and willing to endure scorn to speak the truth out loud.

DAY 304

THOMAS JEFFERSON

"[T]he spirit of the times may alter, will alter. Our rulers will become corrupt, our people careless. A single zealot may commence persecutor, and better men be his victims. It can never be too often repeated, that the time for fixing every essential right on a legal basis is while our rulers are honest, and ourselves united."

Notes on the State of Virginia (Query VIII), 1784

Today Mr. Jefferson might write:

The enthusiasm we enjoy now could change, will change. One day, our leaders will become corrupt and our citizens will become careless. One radical bully is all it would take to start intimidating those more honorable than he is, making them his victims. It can't be repeated too often that the time to legally safeguard every essential freedom is while our leaders are still honest and our people still united.

DAY 305

JAMES MADISON

"We have heard of the impious doctrine in the old world, that the people were made for kings, not kings for the people. Is the same doctrine to be revived in the new, in another shape—that the solid happiness of the people is to be sacrificed to the views of political institutions of a different form?"

The Federalist, No. 45 (as "Publius"), January 26, 1788

Today Mr. Madison might write:

We all know about the ungodly philosophy in Europe—that the people exist to benefit leaders, not leaders to benefit the people. Are we now going to regurgitate that same idea again but in a different form—that the people must forfeit their happiness to the plan of a new kind of political regime?

SAMUEL ADAMS

"It is not unfrequent to hear men declaim loudly upon liberty, who, if we may judge by the whole tenor of their actions, mean nothing else by it but their own liberty—to oppress without control or the restraint of laws all who are poorer or weaker than themselves."

Essay published in The Advertiser, 1748

Today Mr. Adams might write:

We frequently hear people who noisily rant on and on about freedom. But if we watch how they live their lives, we see that they only mean their own freedom—to be legally free to bully those who don't have the position or finances that they have.

NATHANIEL CHIPMAN

"Those who exercise the legislative power must be subjected to their own laws and amenable for a violation equally with the plainest citizen. ...Such partial laws are the first beginnings of an attack on the equal rights of man, and a violation of the laws of nature."

Sketches of the Principles of Government 120-127, 1793

Today Judge Chipman might write:

Those who have the power to make laws must also live by their own laws; just like the common citizen, they are subject to prosecution. ...Laws that give [Congress] special exemptions instigate an attack on the equal rights of all; they are a crime against nature's law.

Day 308

DANIEL WEBSTER

"There is no nation on earth powerful enough to accomplish our overthrow. ... Our destruction, should it come at all, will be from another quarter. From the inattention of the people to the concerns of their government, from their carelessness and negligence."

Comments at a public dinner, May 23, 1837 (Writings and Speeches, Vol. 2, June 1, 1837)

Today Senator Webster might write:

No nation is powerful enough to conquer ours. ...If our ruin ever comes, it will come from a different enemy—our own carelessness, apathy and refusal to pay attention to the issues facing our government.

Day 309

PATRICK HENRY

"Liberty, the greatest of all earthly blessings—give us that precious jewel, and you may take every thing else! Guard with jealous attention the public liberty. Suspect every one who approaches that jewel."

Remarks to the Virginia Ratifying Convention, 1788

Today Mr. Henry might say:

Freedom is the greatest blessing known to man. Just leave us that priceless treasure and you can have all the rest! Protect our freedoms with jealous vigilance; always be suspicious of anyone that even comes close to threatening that jewel.

DAY 310

ANDREW HAMILTON

"Power may be justly compared to a great river which, while kept within its due bounds is both beautiful and useful; but when it overflows its banks, is then too impetuous to be stemmed, it bears down all before it and brings destruction and desolation wherever it goes."

Argument in defense of Peter Zenger, 1735

Today Speaker Hamilton might write:

It helps to think of power as a beautiful, wide river. The river aids the traveler as long as it stays within its banks. But if it overflows its banks and becomes too violent to stop, that river will swallow everything in its path, leaving devastation and misery in its wake.

DAY 311

THOMAS JEFFERSON

"Light and liberty go together. I look to the diffusion of light and education as the resource most to be relied on for ameliorating the condition, promoting the virtue, and advancing the happiness of man. Enlighten the people generally, and tyranny and oppressions of body and mind will vanish like evil spirits at the dawn of day."

To Colonel Charles Yancey, January 6, 1816

Today Mr. Jefferson might write:

*Knowledge and freedom are linked together. I believe the spread
of knowledge and education is the most reliable way to relieve the
suffering, promote the character and accelerate the progress of
humanity. If the masses are informed, the bullying and beating
down of both body and mind will disappear like demons at dawn.*

DAY 312

NATHANIEL CHIPMAN

"Public approbation and censure, when directed to a number
of men, of whom some are known to have acted well, or ill,
but the particular agents are concealed, lose much of their
force. The guilty hide their blushes in the crowd."

Sketches of the Principles of Government 120-127, 1793

Today Judge Chipman might write:

*It doesn't really do much good for the public to praise or accuse
[politicians or parties] as a group when the actual culprits aren't
yet known since the guilty parties can cover up their shameful
behavior by simply mixing in with the crowd.*

DAY 313

JAMES IREDELL

"The only real security of liberty, in any country, is the jealousy
and circumspection of the people themselves. Let them be
watchful over their rulers. Should they find a combination
against their liberties, and all other methods appear insufficient
to preserve them, they have, thank God, an ultimate remedy."

*The Debates in the Several State Conventions on the Adoption of the
Federal Constitution*

Today Mr. Iredell might argue:

The only real guarantee of freedom in any country is for the people themselves to stay suspicious and alert. They need to keep a close eye on their leaders, and if they find collaborators undermining their freedoms—and every other method seems unable to protect them—they've got the option of changing the constitutional, thank God.

DAY 314

THOMAS JEFFERSON

"Weakness provokes insult and injury, while a condition to punish it often prevents it."

To John Jay, August 23, 1785

Today Mr. Jefferson might write:

Weakness invites insults and harm, but a resolve to punish it usually prevents them.

DAY 315

JOHN ADAMS

"Power always sincerely, conscientiously, de très bon foi, believes itself right. Power always thinks it has a great soul and vast views, beyond the comprehension of the weak."

To Thomas Jefferson, February 2, 1816

Today Mr. Adams might write:

Powerful people will always, sincerely and in good faith, truly believe in their own opinions. They will always see themselves as having great benevolence and a grander vision—well beyond the grasp of the weaker class.

DAY 316

GEORGE WASHINGTON

"Against the insidious wiles of foreign influence (I conjure you to believe me, fellow-citizens,) the jealousy of a free people ought to be constantly awake; since history and experience prove that foreign influence is one of the most baneful foes of republican government."

Farewell Address, September 17, 1796

Today President Washington might say:

Please believe me, fellow [Americans], we must constantly be on guard against the devious tricks of foreign influence in government affairs. Both history and our own experience prove outside interference to be a most bitter enemy of a republican government.

DAY 317

PATRICK HENRY

"It is natural for man to indulge in the illusions of hope. We are apt to shut our eyes against a painful truth—and listen to the song of that syren, till she transforms us into beasts. Is this the part of wise men, engaged in a great and arduous struggle for liberty?"

Remarks to the Virginia House of Burgesses, Saint John's Church, Richmond, Virginia, March 23, 1775

Today Mr. Henry might say:

*It's perfectly normal to let ourselves waste our time dreaming.
And, yes, it's human to shut our eyes to a painful truth, preferring,
instead, a comforting lie—until we become captive to it. But is
this how wise men, caught in the middle of a pivotal and cruel
battle for their freedom, should respond?*

DAY 318

THOMAS JEFFERSON

"It has long been my opinion, and I have never shrunk from its
expression... that the germ of dissolution of our federal
government is in the constitution of the federal judiciary—an
irresponsible body (for impeachment is scarcely a scare-crow),
working like gravity by night and by day, gaining a little today
and a little tomorrow, and advancing its noiseless step like a
thief over the field of jurisdiction until all shall be usurped
from the states and the government be consolidated into one.
To this I am opposed."

To Charles Hammond, 1821

Today Mr. Jefferson might write:

*I have long believed (and have never been shy about saying so)...
that the way our federal court system is constructed is the bug
that could kill our federal government... [S]teady and subtle as
gravity, it works night and day, picking up a little power here, a
little more there, quietly expanding its jurisdiction until it has all of
the power and the states have none. I am against this.*

DAY 319

JAMES MADISON

"All men having power ought to be distrusted to a certain degree."

Remarks to the Constitutional Convention, July 11, 1787

DAY 320

THOMAS JEFFERSON

"A strict observance of the written laws is doubtless one of the high duties of a good citizen, but it is not the highest. The laws of necessity, of self-preservation, of saving our country when in danger, are of higher obligation. To lose our country by a scrupulous adherence to written law would be to lose the law itself, with life, liberty, property, and all those who are enjoying them with us; thus absurdly sacrificing the end to the means."

To John Colvin, 1810

Today Mr. Jefferson might write:

Strictly observing the written law is certainly one of the key duties of a good citizen, but it is not the most important. The "law" of necessity, of self-preservation, of saving our country when it is in danger, are all higher in importance. To risk our country by strictly obeying the written laws would be to risk losing the law, itself— along with [our] life, freedom, property and that of our fellow countrymen. That would confirm the stupidity of trading the goal for the process.

DAY 321

ALEXIS DE TOQUEVILLE

"In the United States, the majority undertakes to supply a multitude of ready-made opinions for the use of individuals, who are thus relieved from the necessity of forming opinions of their own."

Democracy in America, vol. 2, Book 1, Chapter 2, 1840

Today Mr. de Toqueville might write:

In the United States, the majority tries to give individuals a stockpile of convenient opinions, thus freeing them from the need to think for themselves.

DAY 322

SAMUEL ADAMS

"If ever the time should come when vain and aspiring men shall possess the highest seats in government, our country will stand in need of its experienced patriots to prevent its ruin."

To James Warren, October 24, 1780

Today Mr. Adams might write:

If the time ever comes when the highest positions in our government are held by arrogant and ambitious men, only the most loyal and qualified heroes will be able to save it from ruin.

DAY 323

GEORGE WASHINGTON

"To be prepared for war is one of the most effectual means of preserving peace."

First Annual Address to Congress, January 8, 1790

DAY 324

THOMAS PAINE

"The man who is a good public character from craft, and not from moral principle (if such a character can be called good) is not much to be depended on."

To John Fellows, July 31, 1805

Today Mr. Paine might write:

A politician who relies on clever spin instead of personal integrity to craft a good image with voters (if such deceit could even be called "good") will be an untrustworthy leader.

DANIEL WEBSTER

"There are men, in all ages, who mean to exercise power usefully; but who mean to exercise it. They mean to govern well; but they mean to govern. They promise to be kind masters; but they mean to be masters."

Speech at Niblo's Saloon in New York, March 15, 1837

Today Senator Webster might say:

There are always men who plan to use their power efficiently, but plan to use their power, period. They are determined to govern well, but they're determined to govern, period. These men promise they will be caring rulers—but they intend to be rulers. Period!

CHAPTER 23

A PERCEPTIVE VOTER

The Greek philosophers Gorgias and Protagorus are credited with discovering—or, at least, exploiting—emotions (pathos) as an effective tool for persuasion, particularly in political debates. Their tactics made them highly successful, wealthy and in demand, largely because their strategy often worked.

Pathetic (lit. "arousing pity") arguments by politicians have worked for millennia and still work today. Human emotions certainly have a pivotal role in forming our opinions on any matter of substance, including political choices. But leaning on emotion to resolve issues with severe, practical and predictable repercussions—leading to more, and often worse, problems—is hardly a wise choice. At least, that was the conclusion reached by our political forefathers.

They presumed, perhaps naïvely, that it was a given that each individual voter would take their voting privileges and responsibilities to heart. They would surely recognize that their choices had enormous consequences for themselves, their livelihoods, their families, their descendants and their communities. And, to be sure, having recently fought hard and endured much for their newfound freedom, most voters of that day knew the adversity that could result from a flippant or naïve attitude toward the electoral process. They understood well the significance of their votes and the unique privilege of that blessing.

Such "gravitas" has waned as those times and experiences have become distant. But our responsibility to study the issues, the parties and the candidates thoroughly and with a healthy skepticism remains a critical and necessary burden today.

Read the wisdom of those who gave us this privilege as they considered the grim consequences of embracing gullibility.

DAY 326

JAMES MADISON

"Knowledge will forever govern ignorance: And a people who mean to be their own governors, must arm themselves with the power which knowledge gives."

To W.T. Barry, 1822

Today Mr. Madison might write:

Knowledge will always rule over ignorance. So, any people that want to be their own boss first have to equip themselves with the intellectual muscle of knowledge.

DAY 327

BENJAMIN FRANKLIN

"A learned blockhead is a greater blockhead than an ignorant one. "

Poor Richard's Almanack, 1744

Today Dr. Franklin might write:

An educated idiot makes a better idiot than an ignorant idiot.

Day 328

EDMUND BURKE

"It is a general popular error to suppose the loudest complainers for the publick to be the most anxious for its welfare."

Observations on a Late Publication on the Present State of the [British] Nation, 1769

Today Mr. Burke might write:

Many people mistakenly assume that those so-called advocates for the people who scream the loudest must be the most caring proponents of their well-being.

Day 329

ALEXIS DE TOQUEVILLE

"The foremost, or indeed the sole condition which is required in order to succeed in centralizing the supreme power in a democratic community is to love equality, or to get men to believe you love it. Thus the science of despotism, which was once so complex, is simplified, and reduced as it were to a single principle."

Democracy in America, vol 4, , 1835

Today Mr. de Toqueville might write:

The most important or, really, the only condition needed to centralize all power in a republic is to "love equality" or, rather, to persuade the people that you love it. That's how the science of tyranny, which used to be so complicated, became simple; it was, basically, reduced to that one, single strategy.

DAY 330

SAMUEL ADAMS

"The public cannot be too curious concerning the character of public men."

To James Warren, 1775

Today Mr. Adams might write:

It's impossible for voters to over-investigate the quality of character of their public servants.

DAY 331

JAMES MADISON

"If it be true that all governments rest on opinion it is no less true that the strength of opinion in each individual... depend much on the number which he supposes to have entertained the same opinion."

The Federalist, No. 49 (as "Publius"), February 2, 1788

Today Mr. Madison might write:

If it's true that all governments rely on public opinion, it's also true that everyone's passion for his own opinion... largely depends on how trendy he thinks it is.

DAY 332

EDMUND BURKE

"[T]he multitude, for the moment is foolish, when they act without deliberation."

Speech on Reform of Representation in the House of Commons, May 7, 1782

Today Mr. Burke might say:

Whole crowds of people instantly become fools when they act without thinking.

DAY 333

NATHANAEL GREENE

"If you would know any man's affection towards you, consult his behavior; that is the best evidence of a virtuous mind. Though a person's professions be ever so voluminous, and his zeal ever so noisy, yet he is not entitled to our esteem, but only civility; for profession is but the shadow of friendship, and saying is not proving.

To Samuel Ward, Jr., 1772

Today Mr. Greene might write:

To know if someone really cares about you, watch what he does— that's the most reliable gauge of his intentions. No matter how often, how loudly or how passionately he claims friendship, he may deserve common courtesy but not respect. Saying he's looking out for you is no more than the shadow of true friendship and doesn't prove anything.

Day 334

ALEXIS DE TOQUEVILLE

"After having thus successively taken each member of the community in its powerful grasp and fashioned him at will, the government then extends its arm over the whole community. It covers the surface of society with a network of small, complicated rules, minute and uniform, through which the most original minds and the most energetic characters cannot penetrate."

Democracy in America, vol 4, Chapter VI

Today Mr. de Toqueville might write:

Once government has successfully completed it's power grab and molded each citizen in a community as it sees fit, they then take on the whole population. In the end, the entire nation is nothing more than a large network of small, complex, detailed and intrusive laws. All people think and behave as told and not even the best and most innovative minds can get through to them.

Day 335

JOHN ADAMS

"In the midst of these pleasing ideas we should be unfaithful to ourselves if we should ever lose sight of the danger to our liberties if anything partial or extraneous should infect the purity of our free, fair, virtuous, and independent elections."

Inaugural Address, 1797

Today President Adams might say:

While we enjoy these pleasant thoughts, we'd be irresponsible if we ever overlook the threats to our freedoms by letting any outside influence or partisan bias poison the purity of our free, fair, noble and independent elections.

DAY 336

ALEXANDER HAMILTON

"Great ambition, unchecked by principle or the love of glory, is an unruly tyrant."

To James A. Bayard, January 16, 1801

DAY 337

JOHN QUINCY ADAMS

"Our political creed is, without a dissenting voice that can be heard... that the best security for the beneficence and the best guaranty against the abuse of power consists in the freedom, the purity, and the frequency of popular elections."

Inaugural Address, March 4, 1825

Today President Adams might say:

With regard to politics, we believe (and I haven't heard anyone disagree)... that the most reliable guarantee of empathy from those in power, and the best weapon against their abuse of power, is independent, transparent and frequent elections.

DAY 338

FISHER AMES

"[The Press] follows the substance like its shade; but while a man walks erect, he may observe that his shadow is almost always in the dirt. It corrupts, it deceives, it inflames. It strips virtue of her honors, and lends to faction its wildfire and its poisoned arms, and in the end is its own enemy and the usurper's ally, It would be easy to enlarge on its evils."

Review of the Pamphlet on the State of the British Constitution, 1807

Today Mr. Ames might write:

The media stalks a juicy story as if it was their shadow (though while upright, they might notice that their shadow almost always lies flat in the dirt). The media distorts, misleads and instigates. It reduces heroism to scandal and loans its ammo and poisonous words to favored special interests. In the end, the media demeans itself by partnering with pretenders. You can't overstate the media's sins.

DAY 339

BENJAMIN FRANKLIN

"Our geese are but geese tho' we may think 'em swans; and truth will be truth tho' it sometimes prove mortifying and distasteful."

Essay, A Dissertation on Liberty and Necessity, Pleasure and Pain, 1725

DAY 340

ALEXIS DE TOQUEVILLE

"But it would seem that if despotism were to be established amongst the democratic nations of our days it might assume a different character; it would be more extensive and more mild, it would degrade men without tormenting them."

Democracy in America, vol 4, Chapter VI

Today Mr. de Toqueville might write:

I think tyranny would look different if it could develop within today's democracies. It would stretch further and appear gentler; instead of persecuting people, it would simply manipulate them.

DAY 341

JAMES WILSON

"Under our constitutions, a number of important appointments must be made at every election. To make them is, indeed, the business only of a day. But it ought to be the business of much more than a day, to be prepared for making them well."

Lectures on Law: Of Government, The Legislative Department, Of Citizens and Aliens, 1791

Today Justice Wilson might write:

Under our [federal and state] constitutions, each election has to fill many critical positions. Certainly, filling them is important enough to set aside a whole day just for that. But, we should take a lot more than one day to equip ourselves to vote intelligently.

DAY 342

NOAH WEBSTER

"[I]f a republican government fails to secure public prosperity and happiness, it must be because the citizens neglect the Divine commands and elect bad men to make and administer the laws. Intriguing men can never be safely trusted."

Essay, Value of the Bible and Excellence of the Christian Religion: Advice To the Young, 1833

Today Mr. Webster might write:

In a republic, if the government can't guarantee the wealth and happiness of its citizens, it's because those citizens ignore God's commands and elect scam artists to pass and oversee the laws. It's not really safe to trust clever politicians.

Day 343

ELBRIDGE GERRY

"The evils we experience flow from the excess of democracy. The people do not want virtue, but are dupes of pretended patriots."

Remarks to the Constitutional Convention, 1787

Today Mr. Gerry might say:

The problems we face are the results of democratic ideals taken to the extreme. When voters abandon virtue, they're easily fooled by phony patriots.

Day 344

FISHER AMES

"I am commonly opposed to those who modestly assume the rank of champions of liberty, and make a very patriotic noise about the people. It is the stale artifice which has duped the world a thousand times, and yet, though detected, it is still successful."

To George Richard Minot, 1789

Today Representative Ames might write:

I always challenge those who humbly claim to be "champions of freedom" and scream highly partisan nonsense around people. It's the same old tired trick that has conned the world again and again. But even when it's exposed, it still works time after time.

DAY 345

THOMAS JEFFERSON

"Man, once surrendering his reason, has no remaining guard against absurdities the most monstrous, and like a ship without rudder, is the sport of every wind."

To James Smith, 1822

Today Mr. Jefferson might write:

Once man surrenders his common sense he has no weapons left to combat the most outrageous nonsense. Like a ship that can't be steered, he's likely to just be blown away..

DAY 346

JOHN DICKINSON

"Heaven grant! That our countrymen may pause in time—duly estimate the present moment—and solemnly reflect—whether their measures may not tend to draw down upon us the same distractions that desolated Greece."

The Letters of Fabius in 1788 on the Federal Constitution (as "Fabius"), April 10, 1788

Today Mr. Dickinson might write:

Heaven, help our fellow citizens to take the time to seriously think about what's going on right now and reflect, with all due urgency, whether the direction they might lead us into may prove to be the same direction that ruined Greece.

Day 347

THOMAS PAINE

"Society in every state is a blessing, but government, even in its best state, is but a necessary evil; in its worst state an intolerable one; for when we suffer or are exposed to the same miseries by a government which we might expect in a country without government, our calamity is heightened by reflecting that we furnish the means by which we suffer."

Essay, Common Sense, 1776

Today Mr. Paine might write:

Every society is a gift but even the finest government is, at best, a necessary evil. At its worst, government is unbearable. Why? Well, though we agonize when we see the same despair in a governed nation as we'd expect from a nation in anarchy, realizing that we, ourselves, granted the powers that have enslaved us makes it so much worse.

Day 348

ALEXIS DE TOQUEVILLE

"'The will of the nation' is one of those expressions which have been most profusely abused by the wily and the despotic of every age."

Democracy in America, vol 1, Chapter IV, 1835

Today Mr. de Toqueville might write:

Calculating and shameless bullies have always thrown around popular clichés like, "It's the will of the people!" at every opportunity.

Day 349

ALEXANDER HAMILTON

"It is a truth, which the experience of ages has attested, that the people are always most in danger when the means of injuring their rights are in the possession of those of whom they entertain the least suspicion."

The Federalist, No. 25 (as "Publius"), December 21, 1787

Today Mr. Hamilton might write:

Thoughout history it's proven true that the rights of the people are most vulnerable when those with the clout to cripple their rights are the ones they suspect the least.

Day 350

NOAH WEBSTER

"[I]f the citizens neglect their duty and place unprincipled men in office, the government will soon be corrupted. ...corrupt or incompetent men wil be appointed to execute the laws; the public revenues will be squandered on unworthy men; and the rights of the citizens will be violated or disregarded."

Essay, Value of the Bible and Excellence of the Christian Religion: Advice To the Young, 1833

Today Mr. Webster might write:

If voters reject their responsibility and put corrupt men in office, it won't be long till the government will be corrupt. ...They will appoint unscrupulous or incompetent men to enforce the laws, taxpayer dollars will be wasted on worthless freeloaders and the rights of the people will either be violated or ignored.

JOHN ADAMS

"When the people once surrendered their share in the legislature, and their right of defending the limitations upon the government, and of resisting every encroachment upon them, they can never regain [liberty]."

To Abigail Adams, July 7, 1775

Today Mr. Adams might write:

If the people ever give up their authority to approve the laws which govern them, their right to refuse government expansion and their power to stop government's intrusion into their lives, their freedom will disappear and they will never get it back.

CHAPTER 24

A SACRED TRUST

The "bottom line" for our esteemed founding fathers was Americans' acceptance and fulfillment of the sacred trust they had been given, by God, through men. Failing to hold their freedom in awe and to preserve their right to vote with absolute urgency would, ultimately, overturn their heritage of freedom.

That sacred trust has been faithfully passed down to each of us. Each generation in between has labored—with varying degrees of success—to conscientiously protect their inheritance and improve upon it for their children, and theirs.

Now it's our turn. And not only ours—what we teach and the example we give to the next generations after us will decide whether the founders' American Vision will flourish or will collapse into the dust of history's bold, but inherently flawed, failures.

In the end, then, it's not the sole responsibility of our elected and appointed leaders to preserve that trust. Their role is, of course, central to that pursuit. But the ultimate responsibility for success or failure in our times—and the proud handoff to our children of the treasure we were given a generation ago—is squarely on our shoulders. We dare not take that task lightly. We can't let it slip from our fingers; the consequences are too grim to consider.

Read these challenging words, written to urge their beloved heirs to grip and hold and squeeze that precious blessing as firmly as they had.

DAY 352

GEORGE WASHINGTON

"No morn ever dawned more favorable than ours did; and no day was every more clouded than the present! Wisdom, and good examples are necessary at this time to rescue the political machine from the impending storm."

To James Madison, November 5, 1786

Today Mr. Washington might write:

There has never been a morning more promising than ours was, but no time has been more turbulent than now! We need wisdom and patriotic examples right now to save our constitutional framework from the coming storm.

DAY 353

JOHN ADAMS

"If the people are capable of understanding, seeing and feeling the differences between true and false, right and wrong, virtue and vice, to what better principle can the friends of mankind apply than to the sense of this difference?"

The Novanglus, February 6, 1775

Today Mr. Adams might write:

If the people are able to understand, recognize and sense the distinction between true and false, right and wrong, good and bad, is there a better foundation on which the lovers of humanity can build their case?

DAY 354

JOHN DICKINSON

"What concerns all, should be considered by all; and individuals may injure a whole society by not declaring their sentiments. It is therefore not only their right, but their duty, to declare them."

The Letters of Fabius in 1788 on the Federal Constitution, (as "Fabius"), April 10, 1788

Today Mr. Dickinson might write:

Whatever impacts everyone should be studied by everyone. People can cripple a nation by not speaking their minds, so it's both their right and their duty to express their viewpoint.

DAY 355

JAMES WILSON

"When a citizen elects to office—let me repeat it—he performs an act of the first political consequence. He should be employed, on every convenient occasion, in making researches after proper persons for filling the different departments of power; in discussing, with his neighbours and fellow citizens, the qualities which ought to be possessed by those who enjoy places of publick trust."

Lectures on Law: Of Government, The Legislative Department, Of Citizens and Aliens, 1791

Today Justice Wilson might write:

It's worth repeating that when a citizen votes for a political candidate, he makes a decision of lasting political importance. He should take every available opportunity to study the candidates for each government office. He should talk over with neighbors and others in his community the qualities people in positions of public trust ought to have.

Day 356

GEORGE WASHINGTON

"It is infinitely better to have a few good men than many indifferent ones."

To James McHenry, August 10, 1798

Day 357

JAMES WILSON

"A habit of conversing and reflecting on these subjects, and of governing his actions by the result of his deliberations, would produce, in the mind of the citizen, a uniform, a strong, and a lively sensibility to the interests of his country. "

Lectures on Law: Of Government, The Legislative Department, Of Citizens and Aliens, 1791

Today Justice Wilson might write:

The citizen who turns a habit of thinking and talking about such issues into a pattern of voting based on his conclusions will develop a consistent, strong and enthusiastic awareness of what's best for his country.

Day 358

JOHN QUINCY ADAMS

"Always vote for principle, though you may vote alone, and you may cherish the sweetest reflection that your vote is never lost."

Uncited quote, The Adams Memorial (dated 1823)

Today Mr. Adams might say:

Always base your vote on sound principles, even if your vote is the only one. If you do, you will always treasure the knowledge that your vote was not wasted.

Day 359

GEORGE WASHINGTON

"If we remain one people, under an efficient government, the period is not far off, when we may defy material injury from external annoyance; when we may take such an attitude as will cause the neutrality, we may at any time resolve upon, to be scrupulously respected; when belligerent nations, under the impossibility of making acquisitions upon us, will not lightly hazard the giving us provocation; when we may choose peace or war, as our interest, guided by justice, shall counsel."

Farewell Address, September 17, 1796

Today President Washington might say:

If we stay united under a competent government our homeland will soon be safe from outside threats. Then we will be able to take a neutral stand whenever we so choose and our position will be fully respected. Then aggressive enemies, realizing it would be hopeless to invade us, will think twice about provoking us. And then we will be free to choose peace or war, whichever is just and serves our best interests.

DAY 360

NOAH WEBSTER

"In selecting men for office, let principle be your guide... When a citizen gives his vote to a man of known immorality, he abuses his civic responsibility; he not only sacrifices his own responsibility; he sacrifices not only his own interest, but that of his neighbor; he betrays the interest of his country."

Essay, Letters to a Young Gentleman Commencing His Education, 1823

Today Mr. Webster might write:

Let character guide you when you choose who you're going to vote for... When a person votes for a candidate he knows to be immoral, he abuses his civic obligation. But, besides betraying his own obligation and interests, he betrays the interests of his neighbor and his country.

361

SAMUEL ADAMS

"The truth is, all might be free if they valued freedom, and defended it as they ought… The liberties of our country, the freedom of our civil constitution, are worth defending at all hazards: And it is our duty to defend them against all attacks."

Essay published in The Boston Gazette (as "Candidus"), October 14, 1771

Today Mr. Adams might write:

In fact, any people can be free if they will value freedom above all and are willing to safeguard it with all. Our freedoms, the fruits of our constitution born out of our fight for freedom, deserve protection at any price, against all dangers. We are now tasked with defending that freedom against every threat.

DAY 362

GEORGE WASHINGTON

"There is but one straight course, and that is to seek truth and pursue it steadily."

To Edmund Randolph, July 31, 1795

DAY 363

SAMUEL ADAMS

"Let each citizen remember at the moment he is offering his vote that he is not making a present or a compliment to please an individual—or at least that he ought not so to do; but that he is executing one of the most solemn trusts in human society for which he is accountable to God and his country."

Essay in The Boston Gazette, 1781

Today Mr. Adams might write:

When each citizen casts his ballot, let him remember that he's not giving applause or a pat on the back to stroke the candidate's ego—at least, that's not what he's supposed to be doing. Rather, he is exercising one of the most sobering transfers of trust known to mankind—and one for which he has to answer to both God and country.

DAY 364

GEORGE WASHINGTON

"It should be the highest ambition of every American to extend his views beyond himself, and to bear in mind that his conduct will not only affect himself, his country, and his immediate posterity; but that its influence may be co-extensive with the world, and stamp political happiness or misery on ages yet unborn."

To the Legislature of Pennsylvania, September 5, 1789

Today President Washington might write:

Every American should make it his highest goal to look beyond his own good; to keep in mind that his decisions will not only affect himself, his family and his country, but that they might impact the world during his lifetime—and determine whether future generations will know political regret or lasting gratitude.

DAY 365

JOSEPH WARREN

"On you depend the fortunes of America. You are to decide the important question, on which rest the happiness and liberty of millions yet unborn. Act worthy of yourselves."

Oration following the Boston Massacre, 1775

Today Mr. Warren might say:

The success of America depends on you. You must pick the crucial answer that will determine the happiness and freedom of millions yet to be born. Make a choice that's deserving of your good name.

APPENDIX A:
THE AUTHORS

Authors quoted in this book are described in brief in alphabetic order below. Days on which their quotes appear are listed following the summary description:

ADAMS, Abigail
Abigail Adams was the prolific and outspoken "first lady" of the revolutionary era and the first American woman to both marry (John) and conceive (John Quincy) presidents of the United States. [222]

ADAMS, John
John Adams was the first Vice-President and second President of the United States as well as father of John Quincy Adams, our sixth president. The senior Adams was an active and vocal advocate of independence as Ambassador to the Netherlands and to Britain. Adams was a delegate to both Continental Congresses, which declared and conducted the war for independence. [29, 63, 80, 83, 87, 98, 108, 114, 147, 154, 158, 185, 209, 217, 218, 219, 257, 283, 297, 315, 335, 351, 353]

ADAMS, John Quincy
John Quincy Adams, the sixth President of the United States, was the son of John and Abigail Adams. He represented three separate Massachusetts Congressional districts, consecutively, and was a Senator before a diplomatic career as Ambassador to the Netherlands, Prussia, Russia and Great Britain, in that order. Quincy Adams served as the eighth Secretary of State under his predecessor, James Monroe, prior to his election as President. He was the first U.S. president to be photographed. [41, 175, 179, 191, 279, 294, 337, 358]

ADAMS, Samuel
Samuel Adams, arguably the most vocal advocate of revolution among the founding fathers, formed and popularized Committees of Correspondence, a network of inter-colony groups to exchange grievances against the Crown. These committees made it possible to unify colonial leaders and led to the First Constitutional Convention. He later served as President of the Massachusetts Senate, Lieutenant Governor and fourth Governor of the Commonwealth of Massachusetts. [122, 128, 135, 197, 206, 210, 214, 226, 237, 255, 261, 266, 269, 281, 306, 322, 330, 361, 363]

AMES, Fisher
Fisher Ames defeated Samuel Adams to become the representative to the First United States Congress from Massachusetts' 1st District. As Chairman of the Committee on Elections, Fisher had great influence on the evolution of that crucial American tradition. During his years in Congress, Ames' advocacy of the Bill of Rights was a key element in Massachusetts' consent to ratify the U.S. Constitution. [215, 256, 272, 289, 338, 344]

BARNARD, John
After an unremarkable military career and years of drifting, Barnard become a Congregationalist minister and a vocal advocate of both economic autonomy and education of the poor. [32]

BLACKSTONE, Sir William
Blackstone was the premier expert on the rule of law in England during the years just prior to the American Revolution. His monumental works, *Commentaries on the Laws of England* and *A Discourse on the Study of the Law*, had a major influence on the designers of the U.S. Constitution, with specific regard to the Judicial branch. [199]

BOUDINOT, Elias
New Jersey delegate and President of the Continental Congress, Boudinot (Boo-dih-NO) was the First president of the U.S. Mint under President George Washington. [201]

BUNCE, Horatio
A Tennessee Farmer who, according to biographer Edward Sylvester Ellis, chastised Rep. David ("Davy") Crockett and Congress for allocating money for charity beyond their Constitutional authority. [15, 25, 61]

BURKE, Edmund
An Irish member of British Parliament and a friend of American independence, Edmund Burke is often regarded as "the philosophical father of modern conservatism." [70, 76, 113, 207, 258, 271, 278, 328, 332]

CARROLL, Charles (of Carrollton)
Known by his birthplace to distinguish him from similarly named relatives, Carroll, a highly successful planter and businessman, was a Maryland delegate to the Continental Congress, a signer of the

Declaration of Independence and a United States Senator representing Maryland. [107]

CHIPMAN, Nathaniel
Nathaniel Chipman was a U.S. Senator representing Vermont, Chief Justice of the Vermont Supreme Court and U.S. District Court Judge nominated by President Washington. [18, 31, 34, 228, 307, 312]

CHURCH, Dr. Benjamin
Dr. Benjamin Church was an early advocate of independence, and a member of the rebel faction known as the Sons of Liberty, instigators of the so-called Boston Tea Party. Early in the War, Church was named the Chief Physician & Director General of the Medical Service of the Continental Army. Although a consultant to the Continental Congress, Church was later discovered to aid the British and was tried and imprisoned as a traitor. [227]

COXE, Tench
Tench Coxe was a political economist and Pennsylvania delegate to the Constitutional Convention in 1789. [49, 52]

CROCKETT, David
Born during the debate resulting in the U.S. Constitution, the legendary folk hero David ("Davy") Crockett served four terms as an elected member of the United States House of Representatives from Tennessee. [55, 60, 67, 242]

de CREVECEOUR, J. Hector St. Jean
Michel Guillaume Jean de Crèveeeour (day kwev-eh-KWAH), also known by his American name, John Hector St. John, was a transplanted French-American aristocrat and prolific writer known for his vivid accounts of life as an American farmer. After returning to France, de Crevece\our took up the cause of black slaves. [134]

de TOQUEVILLE, Alexis
Alexis de Toqueville (day TOKE-veel) was a French historian, social commentator and political thinker. His tome, *Democracy in America*, written during a tour of the United States, examined the living standards, common philosophies and successes of this new American Experiment. [99, 102, 125, 129, 137, 143, 170, 178, 219, 241, 249, 254, 290, 301, 334, 340, 348]

DECATUR, Jr., Stephen
A naval officer known for bravery in action, Decatur served under three presidents and greatly influenced the development of the first United States Navy. [96]

DICKINSON, John
Although born in Maryland, Dickinson, a prominent attorney, was a member of the Continental Congress from Pennsylvania (first) as well as Delaware (second). Dickinson was a signer of the United States Constitution. Following the war he rose to positions as President (Governor) of both Delaware and Pennsylvania. [346, 354]

ELLSWORTH, Oliver
A lawyer and politician, Oliver Ellsworth helped in drafting the United States Constitution. Following its passage, he became a United States Senator from Connecticut and the third Chief Justice of the United States. His proposal to call the new nation a federation of states rather than a "national" government led to the preservation of the title, "The United States." [115, 194]

FRANKLIN, Benjamin
The elder statesman of the American Revolution, Benjamin Franklin never held an elective political office. His role as a Pennsylvania delegate to the Stamp Act Congress, a charismatic wit and charm and his career as a publisher and prolific commentator on political philosophy earned him a position of prominence among colonial leaders. A member of both Continental Congresses as well as the Constitutional Congress, along with this service as Ambassador to France, America's chief foreign ally in the Revolution, forever placed Franklin among the true giants of America's Founding Fathers. [1, 81, 104, 112, 118, 130, 133, 161, 193, 195, 200, 204, 240, 245, 248, 252, 264, 275, 285, 327, 339]

GERRY, Elbridge
A Massachusetts delegate to the Second Constitutional Congress, Elbridge Gerry was a signer of the Declaration of Independence. Following adoption of the Constitution, Gerry served two terms in the U.S. Congress and later become the Governor of Massachusetts. Within a year after completing his term as Governor, Gerry was elected Vice President under President James Madison. [343]

GODDARD, Sarah Updike

A minister's wife, Sarah Updike Goddard became a successful business entrepreneur (Sarah Goddard & Company) and the first female publisher of both the Providence Gazette and the Pennsylvania Chronicle. [293]

GREENE, Nathanael

During the American Revolution, Nathanael Greene served as a Major General in the Continental Army. His greatest success came as commander of the Southern Campaign, driving British General Charles Cornwallis into Virginia, where he would soon surrender to American forces at Yorktown, marking the end of the War for Independence. [333]

HAMILTON, Alexander

Born in the British West Indies, Hamilton relocated to New England to study. After military successes in the Revolutionary War, Hamilton was promoted to Lieutenant Colonel and became General Washington's Aide de Camp. Later, Hamilton's defense of the new Constitution in *The Federalist Papers* earned him a prominent role as Secretary of the Treasury in George Washington's administration. As the first to hold that office, Hamilton had an enormous impact on the development of U.S. economic policies, procedures and commercial enterprise. Hamilton was killed in an infamous duel with political rival Aaron Burr in 1804. [6, 11, 35, 65, 78, 119, 127, 224, 288, 336, 349]

HAMILTON, Andrew

Scottish lawyer Andrew Hamilton (no relation to Alexander) emigrated to Philadelphia. He became known for his eloquent defense of printer John Peter Zenger in a 1735 suit which established truth as a legal defense for libel. [310]

HANCOCK, John

Known principally for his large signature on the Declaration of Independence, John Hancock was a wealthy Boston merchant and statesman. He served as the President of the Continental Congress and had two non-consecutive terms as Governor of Massachusetts. [139]

HARPER, Robert Goodloe
Robert Goodloe Harper was a congressional representative from Rhode Island and Chairman of the first Ways and Means Committee. [168]

HENRY, Patrick
Remembered as a famed orator, Patrick Henry was a Virginia attorney, planter and member of the House of Burgesses. His impassioned advocacy of resistance to British tyranny marked Henry as a prominent voice for independence. As the Declaration of Independence was being signed in Philadelphia, Henry was inaugurated as Governor of Virginia, a post to which he was again elected, after an interim of five years, in 1784. [3, 17, 77, 165, 265, 302, 309, 317]

IREDELL, James
Although employed as a customs house clerk in North Carolina, James Iredell, a native of Great Britain, studied law and wrote *To the Inhabitants of Great Britain*, a persuasive argument against Parliament's control of the American colonies. Becoming a prominent jurist, Iredell was appointed by President George Washington as one of the first Associate Justices of the Supreme Court. [313]

JAY, John
John Jay played many roles in the early years of the United States: New York Delegate to both Continental Congresses and President of the Second, Minister (Ambassador) to Spain and France and the second Secretary of Foreign Affairs (State). Jay was a signer of the Treaty of Paris, the document that officially confirmed the fledging nation's independence. He was appointed by George Washington as the first Chief Justice of the U.S. Supreme Court and, in 1795, became the second Governor of New York. [177]

JEFFERSON, Thomas
Thomas Jefferson, a young Virginia attorney and member of the House of Burgesses, was an acclaimed attorney and author as the call for independence evolved. As a Virginia delegate to the Second Continental Congress, Jefferson was selected to draft the Declaration of Independence with Benjamin Franklin and John Adams. Before the end of the Revolutionary War, Jefferson succeeded Patrick Henry as Governor of Virginia, eventually succeeding Franklin as Minister to France. Jefferson came back to the United States to serve as George Washington's first Secretary of State. After Washington

retired, Jefferson became the second Vice President under John Adams and served two terms as the third President of the United States. [2, 5, 7, 14, 21, 36, 44, 46, 57, 59, 62, 68, 72, 75, 110, 124, 149, 152, 155, 160, 163, 169, 208, 212, 216, 220, 232, 233, 236, 239, 243, 276, 280, 284, 287, 292, 296, 298, 304, 311, 314, 318, 320, 345]

JONES, John Paul

Widely known as a heroic naval commander, John Paul Jones, a native Scotsman, served in both the United States and Russian navies. His legendary victories over British Fleets and fame for his alleged response to a chiding British Office, "I have not yet begun to fight" earned immortality in American historical lore. Jones is regarded by many as the "Father of the United States Navy." [94]

LEE, Richard Henry

A Virginia delegate to the Second Continental Congress who moved the resolution to declare the colonies' independence from Britain; Richard Henry Lee was a signer of the Declaration of Independence and the Articles of Confederation. Following ratification of the U.S. Constitution, Lee was elected as a Senator from Virginia and rose to become the first President Pro Tem of the U.S. Senate. [263]

MADISON, James

A brilliant attorney and "Father of the U.S. Constitution," James Madison was a Virginia attorney, political theorist and, as a leader in the first House of Representatives, champion of the Bill of Rights. (for which he is also lauded as "Father"). A prolific debater with a sharp and often satirical tongue, Madison helped the groundwork for adoption of the Constitution as a co-author of *The Federalist Papers*. Madison served as Secretary of State under Thomas Jefferson and as the fourth President of the United States. [27, 30, 37, 39, 42, 50, 56, 73, 138, 142, 148, 156, 157, 181, 223, 234, 238, 244, 247, 250, 300, 305, 319, 326, 331]

MARSHALL, John

John Marshall served briefly as a Virginia member of the House of Representatives until he was appointed Secretary of State by the new President, John Adams. Again serving less than a year, Marshall was appointed Chief Justice of the Supreme Court. It was here that Marshall gained prominence for his monumental rulings that firmly established the Judiciary as an independent and influential branch of the federal government. [64, 69, 74, 235]

MASON, George

A Virginia delegate to the Constitutional Congress, Mason is one of two delegates (with James Madison) honored as "Fathers of the Bill of Rights." As a member of the Virginia House of Burgesses and delegate to the Virginia Convention of 1776, Mason had drafted the *Virginia Declaration of Rights,* one of the first such arguments, as well as the first colonial Constitution—both of which greatly influenced the *Declaration of Independence* and the eventual *U.S. Constitution.* [54, 82, 131, 192, 225, 230]

MAYHEW, Reverend Jonathan

The Minister of Old West Church in Boston, Rev. Mayhew was an early advocate of a united colonial front against British aggression in New England. His published sermons, including *Discourse Concerning Unlimited Submission,* were read across New England and Europe and, according to some, fired the first rhetorical volley of the American Revolution, outlining an intellectual and biblical rationale for rebellion against the Crown. [90]

MORRIS, Gouverneur

Though a native of New York City, Gouverneur Morris represented Pennsylvania at the Constitutional Convention, where he authored substantial portions of the document and was a signatory of the new governing document. Often recognized as the "Father of the Preamble," Morris was a vocal opponent of slavery. After a term as the Minister Plenipotentiary (fully authorized to act on behalf of his government) to France, Morris was elected to the U.S. Senate in 1800. [103]

PAINE, Thomas

A British native, Thomas Paine gained prominence as an American revolutionary, political theorist and popular pamphleteer. His popular works, *Common Sense* and *The American Crisis* (or simply, *The Crisis*) played a key role in building public favor for seceding from Great Britain. His revolutionary fervor eventually led him to France where he became a vocal advocate for the French Revolution. [8, 9, 79, 85, 89, 92, 95, 136, 141, 146, 151, 172, 176, 180, 184, 187, 202, 205, 251, 277, 295, 324, 347]

PINCKNEY, Charles Cotesworth

A delegate from South Carolina to the Constitutional Convention, Pinckney was a veteran of service in the Revolutionary War and a two-time candidate for President on the Federalist Party ticket, losing first to Thomas Jefferson and, eight years later, to James Madison. Pinckney served as Minister to France under President Washington. [13]

RANDOLPH, Edmund

Edmund Randolph was a prominent attorney and politician, serving as a Virginia delegate to the Constitutional Convention, the seventh Governor of Virginia and the U.S. Attorney General and Secretary of State under George Washington. Like Alexander Hamilton, Randolph had served as an Aide-de-Camp for General Washington. It was his introduction of the Virginia Plan and his role in the Committee of Detail that led to adapting the Plan to a federal government for what was to become the U.S. Constitution. [66]

RUSH, Dr. Benjamin

Dr. Benjamin Rush was a Pennsylvania delegate to the Continental Congress and signer of the Declaration of Independence. Regarded as the "Father of American Psychiatry," Rush was the Surgeon General of the Continental Army and an acknowledged expert in medical theory and practice, chemistry, history and humanities. A devoutly religious man, Rush was active in the American Enlightenment movement and a confidant of Thomas Paine as he wrote *Common Sense*, a key instigator of the will for independence among colonists. [26, 91, 109, 188]

SMITH, Adam

A Scottish economist, Adam Smith's ground-breaking *The Wealth of Nations*, was prominent in the economic theories debated during the early years of our nation, introducing concepts like "rational" self-interest, marketplace competition and supply-and-demand as components of a nation's economic strength. He is called "The Father of Modern Economics" and remains an influential figure in economic studies. [162]

STORY, Joseph

Massachusetts' Joseph Story was a member of the House of Representatives and an Associate Supreme Court Justice. Story is best remembered for writing rhe majority opinion in thr U.S. vs. The Amistad case which freed slaves who had rebelled at sea. [19, 38, 43, 267]

WARREN, Dr. Joseph

An early activist in the Boston resistance to various Parliamentary Acts of suppression, Dr. Joseph Warren was a Major General in the Boston militia and fought in the Battles of Lexington, Concord and Bunker Hill—the initial armed confrontations in what would quickly devolve into the American War for Independence. He never saw the fruits of that war, becoming an early victim at the Battle of Breeds Hill in June of 1775, just two months after the opening "shot heard 'round the world" was fired. [183, 365]

WARREN, Mercy Otis

Mercy Otis Warren (no relation to Joseph) was a highly influential poet, playwright, political writer and propagandist. She wrote one of the first significant histories of the American Revolution and was a frequent correspondent of such men as Samuel Adams, John and Abigail Adams, George Washington, Thomas Jefferson and more. [174, 229]

WASHINGTON, George

Of all of the American founding fathers, George Washington is, rightly, the most prominent and respected hero of independence. An unremarkable officer in the French and Indian War, Washington nonetheless gained a reputation for bravery. Returning to Virginia, he became a wealthy planter and a member of the House of Burgesses. As fervor for revolution grew, Washington was a reluctant convert. When war came, delegates to the Continental Congress selected Washington to lead the hastily formed Continental Army. Washington's eventual success in prosecuting a hard-fought victory and his impeccable character earned him the respect of his peers and his ultimate election as the first President of the United States. His reputation for fearlessness, discipline and integrity clearly marks George Washington as "The Father of Our Country." [4, 10, 12, 22, 28, 40, 45, 48, 53, 88, 93, 97, 105, 111, 117, 120, 123, 126, 132, 145, 150, 153, 159, 164, 166, 167, 171, 173, 186, 189, 196, 198, 203, 221, 231, 246, 253, 260, 273, 282, 286, 291, 303, 316, 323, 352, 356, 359, 362, 364]

WEBSTER, Daniel

Born in Massachusetts shortly after the Revolutionary War had ended, Daniel Webster became a prominent conservative voice in the new nation. A member of the House of Representatives from New Hampshire, Webster eventually was elected to the Senate. A compelling orator known for long, eloquent and soaring speeches,

Webster was chosen twice to be the Secretary of State. But perhaps his greatest reputation came as the leading Constitutional expert of his day, playing key roles in some of the more prominent cases, winning about half of the 223 cases he argued before the U.S. Supreme Court. [86, 211, 259, 268, 299, 325]

WEBSTER, Noah

Known to most Americans as the compiler of the first American English dictionary, Webster was an early advocate of education, text books and public education. He was also a political writer of some note, writing many essays on the superiority of American values over those of England and a vocal proponent of the new Constitution. [100, 182, 190, 262, 342, 350, 360]

WEST, Reverend Samuel

Pastor of the First Parish in Needham, MA, Rev. Samuel West authored an eyewitness account of the British seizure of the Concord arsenal on April 19, 1774, the first morning of the American Revolution. He was a member of the Massachusetts Bay Assembly and participant in the conventions to draft the Constitution of the Massachusetts Bay Colony and to ratify the Constitution of the United States. [84, 274]

WILLIAMS, Reverend Samuel

Samuel Williams is best remembered as a Congregational minister and author of *The Natural and Civil History of Vermont*. An avid adventurer, Williams joined scientific expeditions to Newfoundland and Maine's Penobscot Bay. He taught science, mathematics and natural philosophy (the precursor of natural science) at Harvard. [106]

WILSON, James

A leading jurist, James Wilson was selected twice as a Pennsylvania delegate to the Continental Congress as well as to the Constitutional Congress. Wilson's influence on the U.S. Constitution was significant and he became one of the first Associate Justices of the Supreme Court. [23, 33, 51, 58, 71, 101, 121, 144, 341, 355, 357]

WITHERSPOON, Reverend John

A Presbyterian minister, the Reverend John Witherspoon was a signer of the Declaration of Independence and, later, President of Princeton University. [116, 270]

APPENDIX B:
THE INDEX

KEEP **UP WITH**

goodpoint

P U B L I S H I N G

If you enjoyed and were inspired by this book, you'll want to get sneak previews of coming books in this series as well as other future announcements from GoodPoint Publishing.

It's real simple. Just visit our website at *www.365founders.us* and complete the form to receive advance email notice of coming publications and merchandise.

We're always interested in our readers' comments and suggestions. So, as you complete the form please take a few minutes to share your ideas.

And, thank you so much for reading this book!